How to Make Millions More in Business

52 Timeless Rules to Help You Shatter Your
Revenue Ceiling and Sail Towards a
Lucrative Exit

Gary Beckwith

WP
Wrate's Publishing

First published in 2025 by Wrate's Publishing

ISBN 978-1-917970-08-2

Copyright © 2025 by Gary Beckwith

Typeset and Proofread by Wrate's Editing Services

www.wrateseditingservices.co.uk

A CIP catalogue record for this book is available from the British Library.

To my readers,
You are the reason these words live beyond me.
May this book remind you that stories have the power to
heal, to guide, and to light the way forward.
Gary

Contents

Disclaimer

This book features many anecdotes and true stories.
In some cases, the names have been changed.

Foreword

By Sandro Forte, CFP, FCII, FPFS, Author and CEO of Forte Financial Group

"Focus on the process, and the outcome will take care of itself."

My late father was a successful entrepreneur, and he shared these words with me on more occasions than I care to remember. I would nod along and smile like I was taking it in, but in truth, I didn't really understand what he meant.

At some point during the last 30-plus years of building my financial services business, however, my father's advice not only clicked but I found myself repeating his words, passing the wisdom on to others.

Every founder begins their journey with a spark, an idea. They have a conviction (or at least the hope that they can build something meaningful, valuable and ultimately successful). But somewhere along the way, most of us discover an inconvenient truth: starting a business is one thing but scaling it profitably is something else entirely. After decades of working with founders, I've noticed that the difference between the two is rarely luck, timing or even talent. The people who thrive do so through mindset and by realising the importance of structure and strategy. And that is exactly where this book begins its work.

Let me say a word here about its author. Gary Beckwith is one of a kind. When we met, many years ago now, I was immediately struck by his uncompromising commitment to his business, his team and his family. And as all these things continued to grow, he never lost his warmth or gained a hint of arrogance. The fact that I can now call him a friend is both a personal and professional privilege. So, when he asked me to write the foreword for his second book, I thought of all the things I've learned from him, and I jumped at the chance to help others do the same.

In *How to Make Millions More in Business*, Gary has distilled decades of entrepreneurial excellence into 52 clear and timeless rules. These rules are deceptively simple but not simplistic. They cut through the noise, exploring the behaviours that create momentum, the systems that enhance productivity, the decisions that elevate valuation and the mindset shifts that allow founders to move from operator to architect.

Let them be your compass. Let them challenge you. Let them raise your standards – because the journey to making millions more begins with the decision to think differently and the conviction to act on it. Only then can we push beyond the invisible ceiling we may not even realise we've created for ourselves.

I hope this book helps you strengthen the foundations of your company and sets you on a course toward a lucrative exit. I truly believe it has that power. As a wise man once said, if you focus on the process, the outcome will take care of itself.

Introduction

If you want to drive a vehicle in the UK, you need proof you've reached the minimum standard required to hit the road. If you want to run a business, however, there are no lessons, no theory test, no licence, and if you think about it, that means there's no minimum standard either. What does this say about our attitude to business? How can we trust our own skill sets, or, for that matter, anyone else's? I wonder, is this really the best way of doing things?

On average, people take 35–50 hours of driving lessons to get used to the nuances of both a vehicle and the road. Once you're confident in your skills, you can revise the highway code, learn about 'hazard perception' (for the first and probably the last time), and then sit a test. After that, all being well, you're ready for the big time – the practical! Over 50 sweaty minutes, you'll be expected to drive, parallel park, emergency stop, and actually let pedestrians cross the road.

Assuming you tick enough boxes, and more importantly, you don't do anything *really* bad, like hitting a curb (or a person), you should pull into the test centre and receive a certificate with your name, date of birth and a new license number. After all that, you're done; you've made it. You can peel the L plates from your front and rear and drive at a normal speed from now on.

The experience will have given you a working understanding of, at least, how to start the engine, change gears, overtake safely, stop, reverse and park. You'll know about traffic lights and zebra crossings. In fact, you'll likely have a more up-to-date understanding of traffic regulations than most drivers on the road. You'll be so happy in that moment, you'll probably forget about all the stalling, dirty looks and traffic jams you caused. The stress of the last few months will become a distant memory. No matter how much money you spent, it was worth it. Partly because you know you'll never have to go through it again, but more importantly, because the longer you're on the road, the more you'll realise just how necessary it is.

If *anyone* could get behind the wheel and speed up the M1 without needing to prove their competence, think of the carnage it would cause. Imagine being rear-ended because some 13 year old forgot you had to slow down on a bend. It'd be like bumper cars every time you left the house.

Well, what if the M1 was the economy, and the vehicle was your business? If you have little-to-no understanding of cash flow, budgets, tax liabilities, health and safety, diversity and inclusion, processes and infrastructure, then at the very least, you're clogging up the road. But at worst? Think of the damage you could do.

Sure, a low barrier to entry has bred many a success story (myself included), but it's crushed more than just the dreams of so many others.

Think of yourself as an employee. Imagine trusting your income to someone who has no idea about payroll, pensions, or national insurance. Picture yourself working for next to nothing, trying to get experience in an industry you love, only to work for someone who has zero interest in training you (or no idea how to). What about going to work every day for a boss who criticises you, micromanages, or says inappropriate, unprofessional things at every opportunity?

Maybe you don't have to think very hard; perhaps some of you are in this situation already, and *this* is precisely what drove you to want to work for yourself in the first place. You can never really account for bad personalities, but if your boss had some kind of training, maybe their insecurities wouldn't get in the way of your ability to work together.

You may still be thinking that driving a vehicle is different to running a business. There's no danger when you're starting a company. It's harmless. When you're in a car, you can do serious damage. Well, negligence is dangerous, and ignorance is its irresponsible sibling. From the Titanic to Deepwater Horizon, Chernobyl, Grenfell Tower and the tragedy of the Marchioness, as a business owner, you could end up with many lives in your hands.

"But," I hear you ask, "what if I'm not operating an oil tanker, a 24-storey building or a nuclear power station? Not everybody wants to fill an ocean liner and cross the Atlantic."

Fair point. A faulty product, then. A poorly trained fire marshal. Rats in the kitchen. A badly constructed mezzanine. Loose wiring. An overworked delivery driver who falls asleep at the wheel. Wet floors. It doesn't take much for a passion project to slide into chaos.

And even if your health and safety is on point, or you get lucky and never have an incident, there's more than just physical dangers; people's livelihoods are at stake. When a business goes bust, it can have a catastrophic effect on its staff, customers, suppliers and partners. With limited companies especially, directors can be extremely liberal with other people's money, bankrupting themselves and dozens of others in the process.

Sometimes it's malicious, and at other times, the first domino doesn't even know it is one, but when it falls, it takes a line of others down with it. Your favourite client loses her promotion when you fail to deliver the service you were contracted to. Your staff not only lose their jobs, but they go unpaid. Your suppliers go out of business as their invoices have no way of being honoured.

Hopefully, this will never happen to your business. But they're out there, everywhere. They could be your next plumber, HR consultant, marketing company, or, heaven forbid, business partner. And most of them aren't even acting maliciously; they just don't know any better. Imagine losing everything because someone you've done work for couldn't pay you. It happens all the time.

I'm not trying to paint a gloomy picture here. I love business. I've dedicated my life to it, and so has my entire family. All I'm saying is that there must be a better way. Why should we do things the way we always have?

What if you, we, everyone, were mandated to understand the roles and responsibilities of a director *before* being allowed to start a company? Yes, it would mean learning and passing a test. But what if, once you'd passed, you could show that you have the competence to run a company? That you can be trusted with health and safety, investor capital, payroll and HR? What if you had a baseline understanding of what all that meant? And not just that. What if everybody else did? Your suppliers, your partners, and even your clients. Wouldn't that make the long road of business not just safer but much more satisfying to travel down?

Imagine if you could publish on your website that you've completed a government-signed document that says you're a *class 1 director of a business*. Then, maybe you would launch your company and keep learning and progressing to *class 2* and *class 3*. How many people do their theory test and then, five years later, have no idea what the road markings mean? When was the last time you googled a street sign? (Other than when you've just swallowed a £100 fine).

When you're choosing who to spend your next 100K with, who are you going to pick? A class 1 director, someone who has done the training and understands the basics, or someone who doesn't even think to check their mirrors before reversing? Who would you rather work for?

For black cab drivers, it was called 'The Knowledge.' Before Uber came along, cabbies had to complete "one of the hardest tests to pass, of any kind, anywhere in the world". The Knowledge took an average of four years to pass and meant memorising businesses, landmarks and connections between 25,000 London streets.

Whilst black cab drivers are an obvious example, they're not the only ones. Lawyers, electricians, doctors, accountants, engineers, pilots, personal trainers, the armed forces, all must complete exams before they can graduate into their profession. But, for some reason, a business owner doesn't... yet!

I have an inkling that it's coming. People will complain at first, but it won't take long for them to get on board. Not just because of the knowledge that once they've passed they will never have to go through it again, but because the longer they're on the road, the more they'll realise just how necessary it is.

Preface

I got my driving licence when I was 17 years old. We couldn't afford a car back then, so I needed to find a vehicle to take the test in. My instructor said I could borrow his, but only if I booked a minimum of six lessons first.

It was a clever sales tactic, but for me, it was a nightmare; where was I going to find that kind of money? I lived on a council estate in London's East End, and in the 1960s, that was a tough place to make a living. I worked every hour I could, scrimping and saving until I had enough, and I knew that if I failed the test, it would be a long time before I got another shot. Thankfully, I passed the first time, and it set me up for a lifetime of driving.

If I'd had a similar introduction to business, I wonder if it would have helped me to avoid the early mistakes. If I'd had to sit an exam (and the people around me had to), how much time and pain would it have saved?

Not everyone has access to higher education, and some, like me, don't suit the school environment. But if we were given the chance to learn the basics of industry before going out on our own, surely everyone would benefit.

When I speak at universities and colleges, or at local businesses, I always keep this in mind: What would I want to know now if I were starting all over again?

* * *

In 2006, Ray joined Stemford, a food services business that designed and installed commercial kitchen equipment across the UK. At the time, they had seven employees and generated around £2.5 million in annual revenue.

By July 2008, the managing director had decided it was time for him to exit and offered the business to his staff. Ray and his boss, Richard, were the only ones interested in taking it over. They arranged to purchase the 85 available shares, with each taking a bank loan to finance the deal. By February 2009, everything was finalised, and over the next two years, they paid off the previous owner in instalments.

The business was going well, particularly with large school contracts, and in September 2010, they got what they thought would be a massive opportunity: Three major kitchen projects at the O2 Arena in Greenwich.

It's important to note that Stemford wasn't speaking to the end client directly; they were hired by another company – let's call them *Beyond Measure Design*.

Beyond Measure had already created the plans for the client, now they needed a third party to manage the project and deliver the actual fit-out. Up steps Ray and the team. Working on all three kitchens simultaneously, Stemford were on track to sign off the build on time and on budget. Just three weeks before completion, though, Beyond Measure ran out of money.

Now, picture this: You've almost finished the project, you've invested a huge amount of company time and resources, and all the expensive equipment is already on site. And then, suddenly, there's no more money. Now what? I suppose you'd be okay if you were paid in advance. But what if you'd only collected a *third* of the payments you were due? For a small business, that would be extremely difficult to come back from.

The total outstanding was a whopping £360,000. It was a nervous few months for Stemford, but there was some hope. Beyond Measure eventually found a new owner, Tommy, who stepped in to take over the failing design studio. Negotiations were reignited, and Stemford were offered a settlement. It wouldn't make them whole, but it would cover a huge amount of the damage caused. At least, that was the promise. With £176,000 left on the agreement, Tommy decided he'd had enough and refused to pay another penny.

So, what could Ray and Stemford do? They could threaten legal action, but if they did, they'd need to be willing to back it up, putting even more time and money at stake. For Ray, the principle far outweighed the risks, and Stemford had their day in court. The good news is they won the case. The bad news leads to our first rule of thumb.

RULE OF **THUMB**

Winning doesn't always indicate success.

It turns out Tommy owed HMRC around £1.2 million, and so, the government took precedence over any other claims. So, while Tommy went to prison, Stemford were forced to write off the debt AND pay all their own legal fees.

Ray and Richard worked hard to keep the business afloat, negotiating extended payment terms with suppliers and continuing their work in schools. Despite their efforts, though, the company remained in a precarious position. By the spring of 2012, the financial and emotional strain became too much, and they closed the business. The personal tensions that had built up between the business partners were also never resolved.

I asked Ray what he would do differently if he could do it all over again.

"Due diligence," he said. "We didn't have a relationship with the end client; we were hired by the designers. It was a huge project to commit to without covering, at least, our costs upfront."

Ray was driven by a burning desire to work for himself. He had a tough few years, but ultimately, he shortened his mortgage and learned valuable lessons in business and life. He's now retired, works one day a week in a coffee shop for a charity, and our families are related through marriage.

* * *

I won't tell you that reading this book will protect you from all the bad things in the world. You will come across greedy people, have bad luck, and make some poor decisions, and that's okay; life is about learning. What I do hope is that we can agree on a set of foundational principles, a minimum standard that all business owners can adhere to. This book delves into some (not all) of what might belong in such a programme.

I'm not here to teach you how to send invoices, read balance sheets, or set up email accounts – that's what the course would be for – these pages aim much higher than that. We want to give you an elevated view of all the major areas of business. It should be as valuable to those currently sitting at their desks, ruminating on their dreams of working for themselves, as it is to the seasoned entrepreneur with hundreds of employees and a company gearing up for sale.

Using real-world examples from multi-million-pound businesses, including companies I've started, sold or am currently involved with, we touch on topics that every business owner should know. We tackle health and safety, infrastructure, the importance of processes, and why you need a job description. We talk cash flow, budgets and evaluating stock. We zoom in on buying and selling, whether it's a product or a business.

Finally, we unleash a series of heuristic rules that can be your North Star, a shining light to help you navigate the uncertainty of today's climate and prepare for the world of tomorrow.

Ultimately, we want you to ask *better* questions so you can dig beyond the surface layer to places many entrepreneurs never go.

This book aims to give you the knowledge most people spend a lifetime trying to learn, and in most cases, far too late....

For access to further resources, including our 7-day fast track course, scan the QR code below or visit: garybeckwith.com/millions-resources

Chapter 1

HR

Most companies don't have the HR skills to match their needs.

It makes sense, really, because when you first start, it's just you. Then you employ your mate, his uncle and a neighbour, and before you know it, you're looking at a room full of people you're supposed to motivate, train and, at the very least, pay every month. It gets to the point where you realise it's actually one hell of a responsibility and that your HR solution needs to be a little bit more than just three columns in an Excel spreadsheet for your employees' names, numbers and next of kin.

The typical reaction, especially for small businesses, is to source the most cost-effective option possible. Maybe you find an online HR platform to do it all for you, or you add the role to the office manager's duties. Then you let someone go, and they take you to a tribunal, and all that money you saved at the front end goes flying out of the door every time your lawyer bills their hourly rate. After exhausting many of these solutions ourselves, we hired a top-tier HR consultant, Amy, and it wasn't long before she showed her value.

At first, Amy came in once a week, and we gradually scaled up her hours as the business grew. Of course, Amy cost us more than if we simply shared her responsibilities amongst us, but we always considered it to be preventative; she would make us more efficient and more productive and protect both the company and the employees. Besides, just like an accountant, any good HR person will always find ways to justify their existence. They hold your hand through all the tricky rules and legislation; they take ownership and don't make costly mistakes.

Not to mention, if you are working towards an exit one day, an HR specialist can add zeros to your sale price by helping to set up the kind of infrastructure that allows new owners to hit the ground running.

Job Descriptions

Amy had *plenty* to say about our infrastructure. One of the first things she reviewed was our job descriptions, and she gave us a critical piece of advice that I've taken with me ever since.

RULE OF THUMB

Every duty requiring attention must be in somebody's job description.

As a business owner, you're in for a few sleepless nights churning over problems, solutions and endless possible outcomes. Don't be surprised if you wake up at 3am obsessing about the most innocuous of tasks.

The trick is to not make life harder than it needs to be. Set yourself up to minimise stress. If you're the managing director, for instance, your focus should be on making money and having enough of it to pay everyone each month. You're thinking bigger picture, giving your time to the people reporting to you, what your shareholders are asking for and whether you've delivered the CEO's vision.

These are BIG challenges. The last thing you need is to start getting involved in all the individual tasks as well. You shouldn't be tossing and turning in bed because you suddenly had the intrusive thought that the fire extinguishers may need servicing or replacing. The next thing you know, you'll be driving back to your venue at 11pm in case someone left the stove on.

That's why all this must go into *somebody's* job description. As an employee, you should know exactly what your position entails and what is out of scope. Of course, roles evolve, but as they do, the job description must change with it. If they're not accurate, why not? Who's got 'writing job descriptions' in their job description?

Our office manager, Colin, is the fire warden, and now, thanks to Amy, sitting in his job description, it clearly states, 'Inspect all fire extinguishers every month. Test every five years. Overhaul every ten years.' We have dozens of them, and they've all been installed at different times, so Colin needs to know how long we've had each one and where they are in the cycle.

Now, we know Colin is a fantastic office manager; he's fully trained and knows exactly what his responsibilities are. But, not only that, we have the procedures in place that make it very easy for him to do his job. Colin reports to his boss in his regular one to ones, and everything is documented.

If you do things properly, you can substitute Colin (and the MD, in fact) out of this scenario and replace them with anyone else. So long as they know what's in their job description and are capable of following procedures, you'll be in a good position to grow your company (and put out any fires that come along).

The Joys of Recruitment

Raise your hand if you're having problems finding the right staff. Oh, okay. Let's try again. Raise your hand if you aren't!

That seemingly never-ending cycle:

Hiring -
Training - Resigning

Rehiring -
Training - Firing

Rehiring -
Training - Promoting

~~Rehiring -~~
Oh sod it, I'll just
do it myself.

Finding good-quality employees can seem like a constant struggle, but it's not for lack of options. When a new position opens up, ideally, you want to be able to look at your own people first. It's a balance, though. Good talent will always be attracted to a company that promotes from within, especially in the more senior positions. But since you have to fill the role they're leaving behind, you'll just be kicking the can a bit further down the road. Whatever size business you have, at some point, you'll need to look outside of your own talent pool. But where?

You could reach out to universities for graduates. Schools are always keen to offer employment prospects to their students, and you might just be snapping up someone with a low-price tag, a promising skill set and a burning passion for your work. Of course, you usually get someone without much (if any) tangible experience, so if you're looking for more senior people, this might not be the way to go.

You can jump on LinkedIn or run paid ads on Google and other social media sites. Other than employing someone you know, this is the quickest and most accessible option, and if you have a good package and a detailed job description, you'll get a lot of traction. But that's just it; there is such a thing as 'too much traction'. However good you are with the targeting, you'll be sieving through hundreds of CVs, many of which have no earthly business in your inbox. It can quickly get demotivating when the first person's used size 24 font to fill up two pages, the next lives on the other side of the world, and the next is a 17 year old who has zero experience outside of three Scouts badges and a few months at Starbucks. (There's nothing wrong with a 17-year-old barista, by the way; I just wouldn't make them my finance director.)

Over the years, we tried almost everything until we finally found a solution that worked for us. And that solution (you may be spotting a theme by now) was to get the professionals to do it. In my experience, if you have a good relationship with a recruitment company, they're worth their weight in gold. Kelly Strong was our recruiter for many years; without her, we'd have been facing an uphill battle.

For a start, she assessed everything *before* it even reached us. When you read through enough CVs, everything starts to blend in. You find yourself ignoring the words and wondering why the guy's put a picture of himself on the bonnet of a Ferrari.

Recruiters read CVs all day, every day, because *that's* in *their* job description. People like Kelly can take in all the relevant information in a heartbeat and give us 10 reasons why we should consider each person they send us. They set up the meetings and make sure the candidates come prepared and on time. They ask the right questions, giving us insight into the candidates' goals and helping us to predict how long they're likely to stay with us. They've also got skin in the game. When they're staking their reputation on everyone who walks through our door, there's a real incentive to deliver.

"This all sounds lovely," a voice growls from the back, "but we can't afford recruiters. I've been eating meal deals for a month; I'm not about to give someone five grand for finding me a salesperson I could have poached from the shop floor in Zara."

No one is suggesting you have to do it for every position. But just like having a good HR person, it's a preventative measure. Why hire five salespeople in 18 months when, if you get the right person, one salesperson could be with you for five years?

The cost of recruiting someone goes far beyond popping an ad on a site like Indeed. For a start, your current staff must take time out to funnel through the CVs and interview everyone. A new employee must be trained and acclimatised. Then, just as they start making some headway, they send you an email saying, "Thanks so much for giving me the chance. I love it here, but I'm off travelling for a year."

Now their department is a person down again, so people are back to straddling two jobs. It'll take at least a few weeks to generate interest online, a few more to run the interviews, and perhaps *months* while the desired candidate works their notice. And what if they leave again? It could easily be six-to-12 months before you're back to where you should be. If you were ever going to headbutt a desk, this process could be what drives you to it. Suddenly, that extra two grand you didn't want to part with doesn't seem so menacing, does it?

That's not to say you don't need an in-house strategy, too. It's not *all* down to a recruiter; they're just a piece of the puzzle. And that puzzle will never be complete without considering the personalities you're putting together. If you want *any* chance of hiring the right person, you need the right people in the room. And I do mean 'people'.

RULE OF THUMB

Never hire alone.

Everyone thinks they can hire good staff. They want to be the ones asking the questions and taking control. I wonder how many managers interview candidates but end up doing all the talking. And how many times does the CEO or co-founder walk in late and derail the conversation just so they can show they're the boss?

In truth, hiring is much more complicated than it looks. I never liked doing it, but then, for most positions, it made no sense for me to be involved. You've got to empower your people to make decisions, especially about who they'll be working with. A line manager should know more about who will become a cohesive member of their team than the founder, who probably isn't working with them or even involved in the day-to-day.

You'll be much better served having someone from HR, the line manager of the position, and perhaps someone already working in the same team. (If the person leaving is still on good terms with you, it could be helpful to have them involved in the interviews as well. After all, they'll have the most recent insights into the role.)

If the line manager signs off on Harry because he has the skills and he's already got a good connection with his new colleagues from the interview, suddenly, everyone's excited about Harry starting and what he'll bring to the team. The line manager can't turn around in three months and say, "Well, Harry was never the right person; you've given me someone I just can't work with."

It also means you're ensuring the company's future to the people running it. You don't need to be involved in every decision. You're taking care of the vision; it's up to them to deliver it.

That's not to say you can't get involved as the owner. Sometimes, it's a necessity, but you need to be careful to check your own ego. Just because you hold the power doesn't mean you have all the answers.

I vividly remember a time when my team had done the rounds interviewing for a new Managing Director. They'd narrowed it down from 64 to 32 to 16. Since I'd be working with the MD on a daily basis, it was important for me to get involved at this stage. We refined the list to a final eight and, from there, had a tough decision to make. Then, at the eleventh hour, the head of the recruitment firm threw me a curveball.

"Gary," he said. "I know you're due to make a call on this next week, but I've had a last-minute CV in my inbox, and I've got to say, you're gonna love it."

I looked at the date on my PC. "Well," I replied, wondering if we could afford to push the decision for another few days. "I suppose we can always make time for someone special. Send it over, please."

He was right; I did love it. Dianne's CV made for a

fascinating read, and she had great experience with a major competitor.

I invited her in for a chat, and it just kept getting better. Dianne was practical, interesting, had a great vision for where the business would be in five years, offered insights into optimising infrastructure, and made me laugh out loud several times.

Thankfully, I always follow my own rules, and *never hire alone* had always served me well.

I took Dianne's CV to my colleague, Ken, and slapped it on his desk.

"Forget about the rest," I said, "I've found the winner."

Ken didn't reply. He just leaned over the CV and read every word in silence. Then, once he'd finished, he calmly picked up a pin, reached forward and proceeded to burst my bubble.

"Does this resume remind you of anyone, Gary?" he said.

I closed my eyes for a moment. We'd set out to find a new sales and marketing-focused managing director, someone who could take what we'd built and help us grow the income. What I'd found was someone who would implement processes and procedures and build infrastructure. The thing was, we already had that person.

I looked at him sheepishly. "Me?"

"Bingo!" Ken said. "And I, for one, think you're doing it pretty well."

"Ha!" I scoffed under my breath as I begrudgingly reached for the CV and tore it into pieces.

Dianne and I were aligned in so many ways it was only natural for me to think this person was everything we needed. But she wasn't. We had me, and like Ken said, I was good at being me.

I learned another valuable lesson from that process.

RULE OF THUMB

Never employ in your own image.

We had eight incredible candidates to choose from; any one of them could have done the job, and yet, we could have thrown all the talent in the bin because I'd found my own reflection. It was another reminder to never lose sight of what we're supposed to be doing, no matter how many shiny objects greet us along the way.

The Interview 'Process'

Interviewing is the same as any other part of your business; you need a process. In the midst of a flowing conversation, it's easy to forget some of the things you should be asking and focus too much on your shared interests or whatever leaps out from their CV.

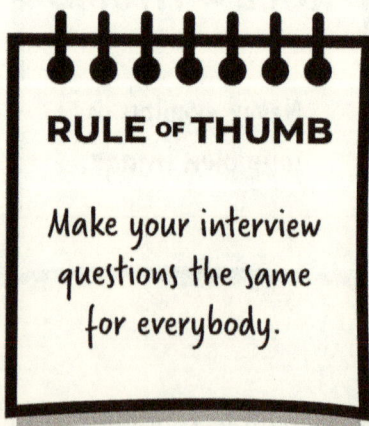

RULE OF THUMB

Make your interview questions the same for everybody.

Create a list of questions that everybody has access to. That way, whoever's hosting the interview has a structure to work with, and every person they speak to will be on a level playing field. If your hiring team has a reshuffle or someone's off sick, it's easy for another person to take over the interview and pick up from where they left off.

When a Hobby Becomes a Habit

If you're going to take somebody on, you need to look beyond their experience and try to understand their psyche. It's not just what they're saying, it's what they're *not* saying.

"What do you do outside of work then, Jim? What's your favourite hobby?"

"Golf. There's nothing better than 18 holes to clear my mind after a long week."

"Oh, great. Yeah, I agree. Bit of fresh air, stretch your legs. What you playing off?"

"Six at the moment, Gary. I'm usually around eight, but I've hit a good run of form recently. What about you?"

"Er... yeah, I've got a business to run, unfortunately."

A friend of mine once joked he never hires anyone with a golf handicap less than 11. If you know how difficult the game is, it's hard to believe someone could be playing off six without it encroaching on their work time. If their phone's always off at 3pm on a Friday or their lunch breaks seem to run four times the length of everyone else's, you know exactly where they'll be.

This goes for being on the other side of the table, too. If you're interviewing for a job, people are reading into everything (and if they're not, they should be). Sometimes, it's best to play things down because what you think might make you look flashy in one area can flash warning signs in another.

Geography Matters

As an employer, you have to understand what people are looking for in their careers. Do they want to be chairman one day? Or are they just looking for a stopgap before they move to Dubai?

"Where do you live, Alex?"

"I'm out in Surrey at the moment."

"Oh, lovely. How long was the journey here today?"

"Just over two hours."

"Any plans to move closer into town?"

"Oh, no. We're really settled. The dogs, you see, they need plenty of space to run around."

If you work with the right recruitment company, the chances are that at the end of the process, you'll have several people who could do the job, just like when we hired our MD at City Cruises back in 2011. We had eight people on the shortlist, and they all might have been successful. Sometimes, these things come down to the finest margins.

Now, I'm not saying someone can't commute for two plus hours. But if one of those eight had to take three buses, a train and a horse and carriage to get to work every day, you have to project that into the future. What does that look like in two years' time? Are they still going to be bouncing into work at 8am, lifting all those around them with tales of a wonderful weekend, or are they going to be dragging their zombified carcass along the sales floor like a battered soldier army crawling through the sticky mud?

Maybe they can work from home a few days a week. Sure. If they're only commuting twice a week, that might have more longevity. But then what? Do they start coming in late and leaving early to avoid rush hour? What if they realise they can get a *fully* remote job somewhere else for the same money? You'll be back to your dreaded recruiting cycle all over again.

"How long have you been in the UK?"

"I just arrived. I really love it."

"What about the family?"

"They're back in Denmark. The kids have just

started at school. I'm travelling back at the weekends."

Wow. That shows a lot of commitment to the role. This lady's willing to be away from her family five days a week and travel home every Friday night. But how does that compound over time? Is it going to get any easier for her? Will she get lonely? Will she miss tucking her kids in at night? Will she end up looking for somewhere closer to home? Where's the longevity in being away from your family?

What if it was the same situation but with a different goal in mind?

"How long have you been in the UK?"

"I just arrived. I really love it."

"What about the family?"

"They're back in Denmark, but we're saving up to bring them over here. This job would be a big step towards that."

Now you have someone who's relocating their whole life and starting anew. What does this look like in two years? Think how dedicated she'll be to a business that helps her and her family achieve their dreams.

Education Comes in Many Forms

In a lot of businesses, they don't care what degree you've got, just that you have one. Why? Education tells you a lot about a person before they show up for the interview. It speaks of someone with a desire to learn, a willingness to sit exams and continue to be trained.

I always advise people that it's a useful route to go down if you can. Having said that, I left school at 15, dyslexic and without a single grade. My commitment to learning came once I started working. I realised I needed specific skills for the roles I was taking on, and I became insatiable in my thirst for knowledge.

If a promising candidate has no education to speak of, there are other things you can look for. Eventually, previous experience might trump education anyway, as you realise that to have risen to this point in their career, they must have been willing to grow and learn. They might also have actual examples of the work you're employing them to do. Perhaps they have certificates in their chosen field, or they're active in the local trade organisations and have their finger on the pulse.

You can even analyse their skills and hobbies. Do they speak many languages? Are they an amateur historian or a grade 8 pianist? And how do you even weigh up this type of commitment to learning against, say, an English literature degree?

Well, it depends on what you're looking for. We joked about a golf handicap earlier, but playing off six shows a willingness to delve beyond just hitting a ball and screaming obscenities when it ends up in the trees. They'd have likely had to play countless hours from horrible positions, braved the rain and the cold, and overcome long periods of being the worst on the course. They've probably done private lessons, watched tutorials, analysed what the pros are doing, and given tips to newbies they've dragged along with them.

You could say the same for a black belt in a martial art. For many, this shows dedication to a craft over several years (sometimes decades). Like golf, you're also spending a long time as the worst in the room, regularly training from terrible positions and taking all the highs and lows that come with it. Unlike golf (hopefully), you might also be getting strangled or punched in the face. By the time you achieve your black belt, you've likely overcome many setbacks and injuries, taught several classes and gained an understanding of how to break down complex concepts for beginners.

Who's to say these are less employable skills than the ability to recite a sonnet or cook a Pot Noodle in a microwave? If you look closely, you can see the student in everyone.

The Acclimatisation Rota

Sally sailed through her interview with flying colours. She lived locally to the office, had ten years' experience, a degree in accounting and was rubbish at golf (that bit's a joke). She was employed in the finance department as a senior manager.

When we hired a full-time employee at City Cruises, they'd have three weeks to acclimatise, which meant before she'd even sat down at a desk, Sally had visited all corners of the business.

Sally spent day one in engineering and day two in HR. Then she headed to our site in York, stayed the night, and went to Poole the next morning. Once she'd met some of the team and got her head around all the various elements there, we brought her back to London. She was an usher on the Showboat one night; the next, she joined the captain on a sightseeing trip to Greenwich. The following day, she jumped behind the bar on an afternoon tea cruise. Then, during a corporate event, she rolled up her sleeves and helped us to load on the production equipment. The next night, she became a customer for the evening and saw it all from a different perspective.

Although it took three weeks, Sally got to see how big the company was; she met people from each department and was able to put a face to a name when they were on the end of the telephone. When she did finally begin her 'day to day', she had much more appreciation for what the other departments had to deal with. She'd seen the chaos on the South Bank whilst out selling tickets, the intensity of a late night on the Thames with a dozen party boats all competing for the perfect piece of the river, and the physical labour it took to work on the store barge and in engineering. It gave her context for why certain issues might come up and a way to rebuff if someone was trying to pull the wool over her eyes.

"Well, I know you have somewhere to put receipts because I spent two days scanning them into Xero."

Once you've successfully run someone through this onboarding process, replicating it is easy. This *Acclimatisation Rota* will serve as a blueprint for the next time you hire a senior manager.

It's important for everyone to buy in. All departments must see the value in welcoming a new face for the day and helping them to understand the business. Building relationships with someone in a different team might seem futile to some employees, but you never know where you might end up. You have to help them understand that one day, perhaps far from here, that could be the person recommending them for a pay rise or even their next job opportunity.

Staff Retention

Hiring people is one thing; hanging on to them is something else entirely.

How do we keep our talent from going elsewhere? You can start by doing the obvious things right: Pay people what they're worth; train them so they can further their careers; promote them; communicate well; leave them alone when they're on holiday; think about benefits and bonuses; host summer and Christmas parties; don't overwork people or go outside of their job description. Ah, there we are again, back to where we began...

RULE OF THUMB

It all starts with the job description.

When people join you, they must understand the package, what their role is and, as importantly, what their role *isn't*. From a detailed job description, they should be able to close their eyes and visualise what the day to day might look like. They should instantly get a feel for what areas they'll already excel in and where they might need training.

This will mean they'll also have something to point back to if their work falls out of scope – and so will you. If they're not delivering on what they promised, you can go back to the job description. Think of it as a blueprint to help them navigate their duties, and, like anything else, it should be reviewed to see what's working and what needs to evolve.

If people are given tasks outside of their agreed role, that's fine, but at some point they'll expect a lift in salary or benefits. When they're constantly having to pick up other people's slack, or you hear words like, "This isn't what I signed up for," trust me, they've had itchy feet for a while.

Have Pride!

How can you make your staff feel proud of what they do? After all, your net worth shouldn't equal your self-worth. Most people want to talk about their jobs with passion and be able to hold their heads high in front of their friends and family.

When we were operating City Cruises, my son Matthew, who was HR director at the time, woke up one morning with a powerful idea. From then on, he decided everyone in the company would address our captains by their titles. "Good morning, Captain", "How was your weekend, Captain?"

It takes many years to become a captain on the river, and this sign of respect from their peers went a long way towards recognising that. It worked so well, in fact, that we rolled it out to other areas of the business. "Yes, Chef", "No, Chef", "Anything else, Chef?" With that simple shift, we recognised their training, the discipline it required and their skills every time we spoke.

Being made to feel like you have an essential place within the fabric of a business anchors you to your position much more than finishing at 4pm on a Friday and boozy lunches with the boss.

If you're in charge of a 500-capacity sightseeing boat, and you're addressed as "Captain" around every corner, how proud would you be to show that off to the people you love? We'd often encourage our captains to bring their partners and kids to the pier so the whole family can see Mummy or Daddy's success.

But pride is about more than words; it's how we feel about what we do and even how we present ourselves. Uniforms might be unpopular to some staff, but they add to the prestige of certain jobs.

Imagine being a sea captain or an airline pilot and turning up for your shift in tracksuit bottoms or yoga pants.

For the employee, uniforms mean you don't have to worry about what clothes to pick every morning. For the employer, it's that you won't have people constantly skirting the grey area of what's acceptable to wear to work. Uniforms help customers know who to talk to, ensuring your business avoids any unwanted brand affiliations or sporting and national rivalries. They're also tax deductible, so they may not be as big an investment as you might think.

A Culture of Progress

If you're working hard every day trying to rise up the ranks and people are constantly being brought in from other companies and filling the roles ahead of you, it can be seriously demotivating.

Our policy was to offer vacancies internally for around a week before they went to the public. Sometimes, our staff would be all over it, but at other times, they might have required a little coaching from their line managers – a friendly nudge in the right direction. The line manager understands what the job takes and whether you have the stomach and the skills to take on the new responsibilities.

You may think you're up against it by applying for

a new role, but think about it: it's much better for a manager to promote someone they know and trust rather than an unknown entity that's coming in from another company.

"You never know what you're gonna get," said the wise and trusted Forrest Gump.

If a manager recognises someone's skills and tells them about an opening coming up, it can give that person the extra bit of confidence they need to apply for it, as it's often only the fear of failing that stops them.

RULE OF THUMB

Communicate early.

It's easy to see the benefits of telling your staff about new positions, but you've got to think about what will happen if you *don't* communicate with them. The last thing you want them to do is go for a job, not get it, and feel like they've embarrassed themselves by even asking. Maybe they weren't ready. Maybe they were *years* away from being ready. But why haven't you told them that yet? Why haven't you let them know what they need to do before they can be considered for the next step up? No one wants to apply for a job only to be shot down or completely ignored by their boss. Now you've got someone who might have been thriving last month but is now demotivated and questioning their future.

As a senior person in the company, you're always trying to get your "worker ants" into management, helping to guide people through the system. If they see this sort of culture in the company, they will join quicker, work harder and stay longer. Don't forget the void, though. If someone goes up, they'll always leave space to fill behind them. At some point, you'll be back to recruiting externally. But, as you've seen by now, if you have the right processes, there are ways to ease that pain.

Over Time, Overtime Becomes Unsustainable

A rota is a science in itself. You're constantly juggling, factoring in new life circumstances and making last-minute substitutions. When you're a young lad in a pub wanting to switch shifts with Kelly so you can go out with your mates on Friday, you might not understand why your boss is so resistant. But what you're not considering at that age (or at that level of experience, shall we say) is that if Kelly covers your shift, she'll be over her maximum hours for the week, so you'll have to take her off elsewhere. Or maybe Kelly can't do it, so she trades with Max on a different day so that *he* can come in and cover you instead. Sound like a headache? Imagine being the manager, especially when you realise Max isn't trained up on the till yet, and this will be his first Friday night.

You've got to ensure that your employees only work the hours they're supposed to. That's easy to say, of course, but when people have last-minute commitments outside of their job, or they get sick, you have to pull *someone* in.

Our best answer to this conundrum was to employ at least one extra person. For example, if we had 20 captains on duty for the day, we'd be paying 21 or 22. That way, when someone was late, sick or just AWOL, we had someone else who could slot right in, and we weren't burdening our best staff with covering for other people's problems all the time. There's probably not a chef or pot washer alive who hasn't had to work back-to-back double shifts because one of their colleagues went out for one too many beers the previous night.

What about the police? Forty-four thousand police officers in London might sound like a lot. But not when you factor in that they're open for business 24 hours a day, seven days a week. On average, an officer might only do 40-50 hours a week each. Then you have sickness, holidays, suspensions, training, court appearances and injuries to contend with. The next thing you know, West Ham draw Millwall in the cup and they suddenly feel like they're a whole battalion short.

If you need 20 captains today, don't rota 20 and make someone work a 12-hour shift when somebody calls in sick. Rota 21 and cover yourself for the inevitable. You know what's going to happen because it always does.

At its peak, we had 512 staff in our business. When you have that many people, there's always someone not at work that day. So why haven't you prepared for it?

Let me guess: The cost of hiring more people?

We talked earlier about the dreaded recruitment cycle. If you have just *one* extra person in a department, you're not left short-handed for months when someone leaves while you scramble to replace them, and you don't make rushed hiring decisions that backfire and cost you much more in the long run.

These extra people gave us the leeway to make good decisions, cover over any cracks, and ensure that, where possible, we could avoid having people working overtime and outside of their job description. In short, anyone with itchy feet was spotted long before they started scratching.

Flexible Hours

ASDA used to win "Best Company to Work For" every year. One of the key factors in their success was how they flipped the idea of "work hours" on its head. Instead of drawing up a rota and saying, "These are your shifts for the next two weeks," they'd actually ask their employees when they wanted to work, and then they'd build the rota around them.

Imagine if you're a single parent, or you're studying or training for a marathon – why would you give up your job at ASDA when they're so flexible about when you can earn a living?

Reasonable Salaries

If you're worried about someone resigning, it's always good to ask this question: How much would it cost me if that position became vacant? Don't just look at how much your employees cost you, but how much they make and save you, too.

If I don't have someone out on the South Bank selling tickets to our sightseeing tours, how much will that cost my business? If that position is becoming increasingly hard to fill, or if people are leaving quickly, it could be that we're just not paying enough. If we can't afford to raise the salary, maybe we need to introduce sales targets and performance bonuses.

And don't just look at the big earners. A cleaner is just as important as a salesperson or a captain. You can't have customers on a dirty boat, and if you don't have cleaners to do it, you'll have to lump those duties on somebody else.

Pay people what they're worth, but whatever you do, don't make it up.

Wage Reviews

Wage reviews are crucial to your business. But that's exactly what they are: *a review* – you can't just make them up.

The following is a recreation of actual events...
I smile as Scott shuts the lid of his laptop. *That was a very productive meeting,* I think. *I must get his opinion on this stuff more often.*

Scott goes to stand up, but something stops him.

He perches on the edge of his seat and gives me the first *deadly serious* look I've ever seen on his face.

"You okay? Is there something else?" I ask, secretly hoping he's not going to be sick all over my desk.

"I need a pay rise," he says. The words were vomited from his mouth so fast they made me flinch.

"Okay," I reply. "Anything else, *or* is that the whole pitch?"

"No, I, erm, I work hard, and so do the rest of the crew. I can't remember the last time the wages went up."

"You got promoted recently, didn't you?"

"Yeah, but why do you have to get promoted to make more money? Surely, as the cost of living goes up—"

"I understand, Scott. It's tough out there. We're above London Living Wage, you know. If I keep putting wages up without a plan, we'll all be looking for a new job."

I can see he understands, but it's not resonating. I decide to change tack. "How much would you consider is *enough* for a role like this?"

He sucks his cheek in for a moment. "I dunno. I guess 20p more per hour. That's what my mate gets. He's cabin crew on an airline."

"Riiiight!" I say. I think about mentioning the contrast in industries: the hours, the travel, and the work conditions, but that's not the lesson here. "You know if I do it for your department, Scott, I'm going to have to review for the whole company's wages?"

"Yeah, I get that," he says, shuffling awkwardly. "Maybe you should! It's only 20p."

He scoots back in his seat and clutches his jumper tightly in his arms. It's like he's sprawled against a tree protesting deforestation.

"Okay, you're right," I say, racking my brains on how I can put this. "It is only 20p per hour. But you know how many hours there are in a day? And how many days there are in a week? Have a guess how much that'll cost us in a year?"

"I dunno."

"Have a guess."

"I really don't know."

I can't just tell him the answer; it needs to really land, or he won't learn anything.

"Okay," I say. "Put yourself in my shoes. What would be an acceptable amount for you to lose every year? Five grand?"

Scott shrugs his lips down like it won't even touch the sides.

I lean forward. "Ten?"

He starts nodding slowly, and, for a second, I worry he thinks this is an actual negotiation.

"20?" I say.

"Yeah, that's about right. You must be able to

afford 20 grand. It's nothing to a business this size. And think of the boost it would give everyone."

I hand him a pen. "Okay," I say. "I want you to work out the following."

He cautiously grabs the biro, peels a Post-it note from the pile and starts to write...

Frequency	Sums	Total Increase
Hourly	£11.20 – £11.00	£0.20
Daily	£0.20 x 8 hours per day	£1.60
Weekly	£1.60 x 5 days per week	£8.00
Yearly	£8.00 x 52 weeks per year	£416.00

"Okay," he says, "So, if we go from £11 to £11.20 per hour, it's £416 per year."

"And how many staff do we have?"

"Eh?"

"Well, it's £416 per year, per *person*, right? So how many staff do we have?" I ask.

"Erm, 300?"

I laugh. "Try 500!"

He clenches his teeth. "I'm gonna need a calculator for that."

"Me and you both, Scott."

He gets his phone out and starts tapping away. Then his eyes light up. "Hang on," he says, hitting the AC button and starting again. "That can't be right."

I lean forward slightly.

"Use 512 this time," I say. "That's how many staff we have at the moment."

He types '416 x 512 =' then, almost immediately, he clears it again, rechecking the Post-it note. This time, he keeps pressing clear until he's positive it's back to zero, and then he slowly punches in each digit.

"£212,992!" I say before he's finished. "You were right the first time."

He fires me a sceptical look. "I thought you needed a calculator."

"It's not the first time I've done the maths, Scott." I stand up and walk around to his side of the table. "If I increase everyone's wages by just 20p per hour, it'll cost us almost a quarter of a million pounds. Let's say you own this business one day. How much is too much?"

"Yeah, I get you," he says, dejected. "That's definitely too much."

"Do you like your job?" I ask.

"Yeah. You know I do, I love it."

"Are you learning?"

"All the time!"

I go to speak again, but he interrupts.

"And... I've been promoted twice in two years. I'm

earning much more than when I started. I'm listened to."

"What about your mate? Does he like his job on the airplanes?"

"Not really. He's constantly moaning, to be fair," Scott says, suddenly looking more sheepish than when he started. "Sorry, I *am* grateful, it's just—"

I raise my hand to stop him. "You never have to worry about asking for something," I say, patting him on the back. "I just want you to see the bigger picture. I'd love to pay you all what you want, but there's a structure for a reason. If I just cave when people ask me for more, it won't be long before I can't give them anything at all."

Scott smiles, putting out his hand to shake mine. "Thanks, Gary," he says. He walks towards the door and opens it. "And just so you know," he adds. "I'd never leave you for an airline, even if they were paying double."

I laugh. "Thanks, Scott, you're more loyal than most, then."

"Not really," he replies. "I'm scared of flying."

* * *

Paying people what they're worth is crucial, but you need to figure out if you can afford it first. Where is that money coming from? At the moment, you might make a £1 million a year in profit. If you increase your wages 200k, that's a huge chunk of it evaporating at the press of a button. You may not have 500+ employees, you may only have 30, but it's all relative. In fact, the smaller you are, the more you're likely to notice.

RULE OF THUMB

Don't (ever) make it up.

Before you contemplate a wage rise, there's work to do. Consider your prices. Can you put them up? If so, by how much? Are you regularly out of stock because you're in such high demand? Have you looked at the industry standard? Are your costs below your competitors? Are you confident enough in your service that you don't have to price match anymore? Can you be the premium option?

What about your costs? Do you need this many staff? Can you consolidate some roles and use the extra cash to spread amongst the rest of the team? This might be a solid option, but if you've got ambitious expansion plans, it might stop you in your tracks.

You need to create a framework that guides you in your decision-making. If you're recruiting for an assistant manager, the salary band might be £30,000– 34,000 per year. Maybe you really like this candidate you've just interviewed, and you'll do anything to land them. The problem is the company up the road has offered her £36 grand. Do you match it? Is that setting a precedent for the role? And what about the other roles around it? Will these staff suddenly expect more money?

It's no different to negotiating with a customer; sometimes, you've got to move people away from price. Guide them towards all the things you can offer as a package outside of salary: performance bonuses, health care, a company vehicle, training, promotion opportunities, experience, or company culture. Maybe, on this occasion, the answer is to raise the salary band. The point is that you can't just start making it up. Don't say yes on a whim because you're the CEO and you can make the big decisions on the spot. It's *so* important to get the budget right. If you don't, it could all come crashing down very quickly.

Your assistant manager is in a salary band. Once they reach the top of that, they can't get any more until they move up to the next position. It's the same for everyone. If someone's answering customer queries in the call centre, they're in one category; if and when they become a supervisor, they move up to the next band. That's how it works. You've got to set these parameters and stick to them until you've done your research. Get away from the cost per person and department. Zoom out and look at the business as a whole, then zoom out further and assess the industry, then do it again and look at the economy. The more information you have, the better equipped you'll be when you zoom back in again.

The Departure Lounge

No matter how much money you throw around, how legendary your Christmas parties are, or how much they buy into your vision, it's rare for people to spend their whole career with you. There are an indefinite number of reasons why people might resign, and you can tear your hair out trying to understand people's motives.

All that matters is they're doing what they think is best for them and their family. So, when they decide to move on, you *can't* take it personally. No matter how you feel about them leaving, they've invested part of their life in your dream, so it doesn't take much to send them off with a pat on the back.

"Thank you for all your hard work. I wish you well. Please keep in contact and let us know if you have any problems in the future."

Nice person? Good karma? Maybe. But it's not just about you and them; it's just as crucial for the employees who are staying. They're always listening and, no doubt, still talking to ex-colleagues, some of whom will have become their close friends. The last thing you want is for people to influence morale after they've already left.

Running a business can be like creating your own little *Coronation Street*. Every day, people laugh, cry, fight, compromise, fall in love, blow things out of proportion, and overcome seemingly impossible odds (and a large chunk of that will have nothing to do with the job). It's all so close-knit; no matter how hard you try, home dramas will often find a way inside the company walls. There's no way to hide it under the rug, so you may as well give people the space to be themselves.

Most days, I'd go around and talk to the staff about their personal lives. I already knew about their work lives; I'd see them every day. I wanted to know how the kids were and what TV shows they were watching.

"Is Tommy still playing the violin?" / "Where are

you holidaying this year?" / "Luton were rubbish last night, weren't they?"

People are proud of their families, and given the chance, they love to talk about them. As a boss, if you make an effort to remember the little things outside of work, when the big things come around, your team are much more likely to feel safe, supported and able to face any challenges that lie ahead.

Don't Fall at the Final Hurdle

"So, how much did they steal again?" you say.

Your HR manager turns to the Head of Ticketing, who shoots another glance at her notes and takes a deep breath. "Our best estimate is about £1,200," she says.

"Right. Okay," you reply. "Well, we can talk about how that was possible in another meeting, but for now, let's focus on what we're here for. If he's stealing that amount, it's unlikely to be his first time, isn't it?"

The HR manager shrugs his lips down. "Well, he got away with it for a while, so you'd assume he's had some practice, that's for sure. He was quite slick."

You turn your head and peer out the window for a moment, gathering your thoughts.

"Hmm. What did his references say, then? Surely, he's left a trail of misdeeds behind him."

When the silence lingers for a moment too long,

you spin your head back. Both managers have sunk lower in their chairs.

"You *did* contact his references?" you say.

"I, er..."

They exchange glances, and the room falls into another hush.

"Okay," you say, scratching your head. "I think we've got some work to do."

* * *

If you've undergone a lengthy recruitment process, it would be a shame to fall at the final hurdle. Make sure you hear from their former employers. For all you know, they've vastly exaggerated (or even made up) what's on their CV.

Now, by law, an employer *can* give a former staff member a bad reference, but it rarely happens. I know this seems strange, but giving a negative response can open the company up to all sorts of legal claims, where they may be forced to prove what they said was fair and accurate. It's a headache you just don't need. Besides, how do you regulate what the managers say, especially when emotion is involved?

"Oh, what, Jimmy? Nah, he was rubbish. You'd be better off hiring a turnip; they're much more amusing and probably last longer under pressure."

To avoid the drama, companies tend to have a blanket policy of refusing to give references for bad leavers. So, if you call someone, hoping to hear all about Jimmy's exploits, but they won't tell you *anything* about him, *that* speaks volumes. Perhaps you try his next contact, but they only give you his start and finish dates. Now Jimmy's beginning to feel like a risk, isn't he?

It's worth making the effort, because, at the very least, you'll get nothing back, which always tells you something. On the flip side, you might just get a ringing endorsement.

"Jimmy was great. He's very ambitious, we just couldn't give him that next step up. We'd be delighted to see him land somewhere that fits his vision for the future."

Now, confidence in Jimmy begins to grow.

Contacting references is almost a forgotten practice. People seem to assume that if someone's able to provide a list of names, they must all have good things to say. Or perhaps you got on with them so well in the interview that you think there's no chance they'd lie about it. But, if you've ever had the misfortune to run into a con artist, you'll know they're some of the most likeable people you'll ever meet. They wouldn't get very far if they weren't. You have to do your due diligence with everyone, from staff to investors, business partners, clients and suppliers.

Speak to their network. Check their online presence. Make sure they are who they say they are.

You're Fired

Not everyone will be pulling in the same direction all the time. Some people do everything they can to resist change, while others might sabotage their colleagues' work to elevate their own. There are blockers who slow things down and clog up the pipeline. You get bad apples who spread negativity and misinformation. You might even have managers who bask in their own egos, restricting people's progress and taking advantage of their position.

My advice is to quickly remove anti-changers, saboteurs, blockers, bad apples and poor managers. But before you fire anyone, there's something you need to do. They say the truth hurts, and this one's about to *sting:* You must look at yourself first.

If you had to let someone go before they could demonstrate their potential, it says as much about your processes as it does about the individual.

It stands to reason that the more accurately you recruit, the less time and money you'll spend clearing up the mess. But no system is fool proof. So, every time you let someone go, you must analyse why, and use that knowledge to improve your processes. Whether they lasted 10 minutes or 10 years, it's time for some tough questions. How did we get here? And what can we change internally to reduce the risk of it happening again? Start at the beginning. What did the job description say? Who did the interview? Were the right people in the room? Who checked the references? When did you first notice a slip in their performance? What did you do about it?

RULE OF THUMB

If you fire someone
it's your fault.

If you haven't already, implement regular one to ones with every team member. Make sure their line manager is there, and ideally someone from HR. Have someone take notes so you can refer back to them next time. Everything needs to be written down.

If you have all these processes in place, it's extremely rare that you'll have to fire someone out of the blue. You'll see it coming. You'll be able to adapt and readjust their goals and targets.

Go over the job description, company handbook and employment contract with them. Make sure they understand what their role is. How can they underperform if there are no indicators for what a good performance is?

Perhaps they just need a break or more training, or perhaps they have gotten sick and tired of staring at spreadsheets all day. Can you shift them to a different department where they get a new lease of life or gel better with the team? Maybe this role just isn't for them anymore. Keep communicating, help them make their decision, and if you part ways, do it mutually.

If none of that is working, it's time to cut your losses. Go over those same three documents (job description, company handbook and employment contract) and point out the places they need to improve. So long as you have the correct information, you'll be able to follow the procedure for dismissal. Have a legal professional review your contracts; you want them watertight, because one day it will matter.

In the meantime, just make sure you're keeping records. If someone is consistently late every morning, make a note of it, bring it up in the one to ones, and send them an email summarising what you talked about. Take them through the disciplinary process and paint them a picture of the different paths they have in front of them.

Amicable is always best. But sometimes things can turn nasty. If you have someone who is really damaging to the company, you have to get them out. You can follow your procedure to the letter and still end up in a tribunal. It happens. Put some money in the budget every year, and don't let it get you down. Use the experience to learn from, improve your processes and tighten your contracts, and keep moving forward.

Psychometric Testing

Earlier in this book, we discussed the importance of understanding a candidate's psyche in the interview process. They may be able to answer every question flawlessly, but it's up to *us* to establish the critical information that lies *beyond* their answers: Will they fit into the team? How are they with conflict resolution? What are they *not* saying?

Many businesses know this, so they put a lot of emphasis on finding the right questions to ask in an interview. But the thing is, once you've hired someone, understanding what makes them tick becomes even more crucial.

Psychometrics is a field of psychology that assesses 'mental capacities and processes'. The two general tests focus on *cognitive ability* and *personality*, offering insights into people's performance, competence and motivations.

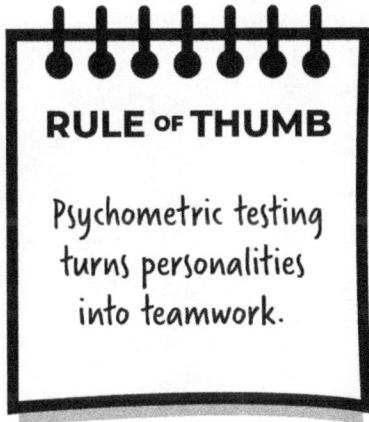

> **RULE of THUMB**
>
> Psychometric testing turns personalities into teamwork.

Our goal was to get our people to collaborate better, and so by understanding their personality types, we hoped to find out more about them and identify who they were most compatible with. It turned out to be one of the most beneficial things we ever did for our team dynamic.

For around 10–20 minutes, each staff member answered questions carefully designed to help uncover their dominant personality traits. Once they were finished, they were assigned a colour. Each colour grouped these traits together and represented a person's dominant behaviours. If you were RED, for example, you were strong-willed but lacking details. If you were YELLOW, you were organised but indecisive.

Check out the graph below and have a think about what colour you might be.

RED	YELLOW	BLUE	GREEN
Strong-willed	Creative	Precise	Analytical
Confident	Dynamic	Patient	Relaxed
Entrepreneuial	Sociable	Organised	Caring
Lack of details	Disorganised	Indecisive	Overcritical
Dominating	Easily distracted	Overcautious	Impersonal

How it Helps!

At one of our senior management meetings, we invited Peter, our psychometric tester, to run some further training. The first thing Peter did was to ask everyone to share which colour they were, and after a quick chat, he singled out four people to take part in an exercise. The rest of us then sat quietly and observed while those four took centre stage.

I can't remember the task now – probably because that's not the point of the exercise – but essentially, they were asked to work as a team to solve a problem. They were given one hour to complete it; if they didn't, the penalty was death. (A bit harsh, I thought).

The hour came and went, and they failed spectacularly – still, it was nice knowing them.

Whilst this was clearly a game, it was given the reverence it deserves. No one wanted to die – in role-play or otherwise – especially in a room full of their peers. Unfortunately, they were utterly hopeless. Soon after, Peter told us that no one ever actually solved the task, and the four breathed a collective sigh of relief. (Which was funny because, as I pointed out at the time, that was the first thing they'd actually done together.)

Before we started, it seemed like Peter had picked the players at random, but in fact, he had selected one person from each colour grouping. The point he was illustrating is that unless people understand what they bring to the table, it's very difficult for a group to reach its potential. In this scenario, they needed someone with an analytical mind to come up with the plan. GREEN would have been the logical choice, but when RED decided to take the situation by the scruff of the neck, GREEN was overpowered. GREEN tried going to BLUE for some support, but BLUE couldn't deal with the aggro. Meanwhile, YELLOW was too busy balancing on one chair leg to follow what was going on. As a result, none of them ended up working to their strengths, and they all tragically died.

As entertaining as this may have been in our safe

office environment, it's not all fun and games for some people. In certain jobs – the armed forces, the police, paramedics – a lack of teamwork really can mean life and death. But then, if you think about it, it can mean life and death for your business, too.

Building successful teams is a puzzle, and the more information you can bring to the equation, the easier it is to find a solution. It's a constant balancing act between various personalities. With the help of psychometric testing, we could go beyond face value and gut feeling and start delving more into actual data.

If I'm trying to build a finance team, I might pick four BLUES and one GREEN, as together they would bring a healthy mix of analytics, caution, patience, precision and organisation. What I can't have is three REDs and two YELLOWs, who would be a steaming cauldron of strong wills, distraction, socialising and domination. Having said that, on the sales floor, I could see that being a recipe for success.

Whilst this process no doubt improved our productivity and office culture, there were individual stories that stuck with me, too. I remember when Tom, one of our captains, pulled me aside and told me what he'd learned.

Tom's boss, Eric, had a very annoying habit. Every time he asked Tom a question, he would pick up an imaginary remote control and pretend to forward him. This made Tom so anxious that he rushed to get to the point and found himself tripping over his words.

Their conversations used to go like this:

Eric: "How come Lucy isn't in today?"

Tom: "Well, she's not been well all week. And yesterday, I told her to play it by ear when she woke up. I think she got dressed and decided she was too ill. She phoned in this morning, and I just said, 'Take the rest of the week; we don't want you getting anyone else sick, do we?' I'm sure she'll be back on Monday."

By this point (if not long before), Eric would either be suppressing a yawn or using his remote to try and move the conversation along. After psychometric testing, though, it all became clearer. Eric was a RED; he didn't care about the details, he just wanted to remove all the fluff and skip to the facts.

So, Tom started to take the hint (and the initiative):

Eric: "How come Lucy isn't in today?"

Tom: "She's got the flu."

That was it. Eric no longer had time to even pick up the remote, and for Tom, communication had never been so easy.

* * *

Think about the last time you had a problem with a colleague at work. When you got home, maybe you just wanted to unload all that stress onto someone. So, you grabbed your housemate and started telling him all about what your colleague did and how rude she was. All you wanted was someone to listen, agree with what you were saying and maybe, depending on how close you are, lean in for a hug. You're a great listener, and if it was the other way around, that's exactly what you'd do, so it's not too much to ask.

The problem is, you've gone to Mr Fixer, haven't you? He starts telling you how you could have approached the situation differently, that your colleague might have got the wrong end of the stick and that maybe you should freshen up your CV if you're that unhappy.

Now you're even more annoyed because he "Never takes your side" and he "Never bloody listens." Psychometric testing won't make people who you want them to be, but if you can start understanding personality types, you can navigate these situations without adding to your stress levels. Next time you're frustrated and need some help, you can go to your housemate. When you just want a moan and a cuddle, give Katie a call, because she loves nothing more than a cup of tea and a gossip.

Having access to training that transcends the workplace is extremely rewarding for everyone involved. Not only can they apply their knowledge in the office, but they can use it to make their lives better. As we've already established, there's a *significant* cost to a business every time you change personnel. Adding this type of testing can minimise the risk of getting the wrong people, ensure the right people stick around for longer, and, at the very least, help us all to understand why some friends never seem to respond exactly how we want them to.

Chapter 2

Infrastructure

Staffing Levels

Harry from the sales department wants to leave. It's a shame because he's been with us for a few years now. He's made lots of money for himself (and the business), and we've loved having him around. His manager can't believe it; she's shocked, and *that* is why I'm shocked.

We employed 512 people (don't worry, you're about to see why I keep being so specific with that number). With that many personalities, it's not unreasonable to assume *at least* one person will leave every month. As for Harry, he's in the sales team, which is particularly volatile, so the turnover is usually slightly higher there than in other departments.

Knowing all of this, do you think it's good business for us to wait until Harry hands in his notice before we start recruiting? Why didn't we know he was going to leave? Harry might have kept his cards close to his chest, but that's not an excuse. Somebody *will* move on, whether his name is Harry or not, because they always do. So, why weren't we prepared for it?

In truth, our company could have operated with 500 people, maybe less, but running a business like that is similar to having just enough income to pay your bills every month but zero savings. You're constantly on edge until, one afternoon, you stop sucking on your Chupa Chup and decide to bite into it instead. You hear a loud crack, and you hope to God it's the candy crushing, but in your heart, you know it's not. A few days later, you're desperately trying to scrape together a grand for the dentist just so you can sleep at night without agonising tooth pain.

Five hundred roles means employing 512 people. Think of that extra 12 staff as your life savings. They don't just sit there doing nothing; they're an investment, and while they still contribute to your income, you'll see your biggest return if anything goes wrong (and it always does). In that situation, you can just delve into the pot, pay for your root canal and get on with your life.

Now, you might be thinking, *We can't afford to have*

a surplus of staff. But you must look at the bigger picture and ask yourself the question: *Can you afford not to?*

If you need a minimum of 500 people to run your business effectively, in one month, how many of those could be off sick, on maternity or paternity leave, retiring, resigning, AWOL, injured, struggling with mental health, on training, on holiday, at a seminar, tired and wired from the weekend, only just hired, about to be fired, caught in traffic, having family troubles, at a funeral? The. List. Goes. On. (And on and on.) With so many reasons why you could be shorthanded, if you don't plan for it, you'll be running a business that is *never* at full strength.

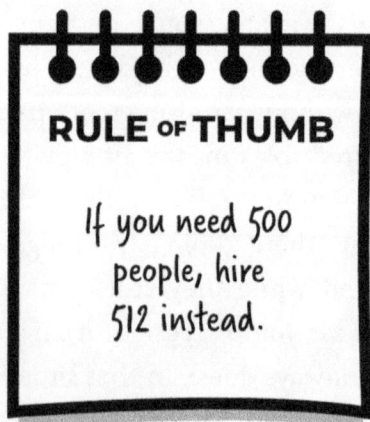

RULE OF THUMB

If you need 500 people, hire 512 instead.

Sure, sometimes, you might have an extra set of hands or two looking for things to do. But as soon as someone has a day off, turns up late, or gets sick, you've already made up for it because you can still operate with a full team.

If you have 10 coaches carrying passengers every Saturday, don't rota 10 drivers. All you need is *one* person to phone in sick, and all of a sudden, you're a coach down for the day. How much is *that* going to cost you, both financially and in reputation? Is there a one in 10 chance someone could be late or off sick today? That doesn't seem like a crazy bet, does it? What about next week? Or the week after? You know it's going to happen, so don't fail to plan for it and then get annoyed when it does.

We don't do this *just to* cover for people, either. Think how much more efficient your teams can be when they reduce their workloads, how much more time and care they can put in, and how this will lead to better job satisfaction, fewer mistakes and a more impressive final product. You're not being forced to burden people with a bunch of tasks outside of their job description either.

"Tom, Harry's left, so I need you to make 75 cold calls a day, on top of all the quotes and site visits, please. Just until we replace him."

"Oh, not again!" Tom says, hanging his head.

"Are you part of the team or not, Tom?" I say.

"No worries, boss, you can count on me," he replies, as he surreptitiously opens his CV and starts adding his latest experience.

If you want to retain your staff, you can't keep doing this to them. You've got to let them work within their role, and if the parameters must change, so should their compensation. When people work longer hours, especially without being paid for the privilege, they begin to feel like all they do with their lives is wake up and work. They make uncharacteristic mistakes that knock their confidence, and it may not be long before they start resenting their job. They end up taking their stress home with them, which only compounds overnight and comes right back into work with them the next morning.

An overstretched department is on the brink of collapse, and it usually only takes one link to break the chain; one person leaves, and it sparks an exodus.

If you have extra hands on deck, it allows you to train people properly, bed them in (remember the acclimatisation rota), and not chuck them straight in at the deep end. If Harry does leave and you rush to replace him, you can't just throw a new recruit in with a bunch of personalities that don't fit. Why did you do your psychometric testing if you're not going to use it?

RULE OF THUMB

You recruit better when you're not panicking.

So, give yourself some leeway. Senior people often have a three-month notice period before they can join you. What if they say yes and then change their mind after month two? Or, worse still, what if they start working for you, only for everyone, including them, to realise they're not right for the job within the first month? If they leave, it could realistically be six months after you started recruiting that you manage to fill the role, and by that point, you'll be tempted to stick in anyone who's even remotely capable.

As businesses grow, your recruitment strategy becomes even more integral. You can't always get it right, but you *have* to be prepared.

My advice is to have someone review the attrition

rate every year. How many P45s does your company issue on an annual basis? You should know this number at the start of each year, so when Harry hands in his notice, while it might be disappointing, it's *never* a shock, and – for those of you that got your Scouts badges – you should always be prepared for it.

I believe that 95% of what you do as a business owner is build infrastructure; the other 5% is the actual product or service you're selling. You could be making balloons, running an airline, or building widgets; the mechanics behind the scenes are very similar. HR is the same for any company. It's getting the right staff in the right job, having them trained and retrained, and contributing more to the business than they cost.

RULE OF THUMB

Every employee should generate £100,000 t/o.

That means if you have 30 staff, your turnover should be north of three million pounds. If it's closer to two million pounds, in theory, you need to let 10 people go. Similarly, if you have 20 people in a three-million-pound company, maybe you can afford to grow. This is, of course, industry specific. A tech company is likely to have a higher *Revenue per Employee* than a clothing manufacturer. Speak to your accountant and find out what the average is in your industry. With some basic maths and simple restructuring, you can often make a conscious choice between profit and loss.

Rather than operating on assumptions, work out the cost of employing extra people versus the implications of always being short-staffed. Figure it all out and put it in the budget. And the next time you think you can't afford something, remember to check if you can afford *not* to have it.

Physical Infrastructure

If you plan to grow your business, staff retention should always be a priority, but don't forget to think about how you can attract new talent. It's not just about the salary or bonuses, or even the fancy company car and the big clients they get to work with. What does it *feel* like on a daily basis? Will they be at home by themselves all day? Or are they in the office from 8am to 6pm? What's the vibe in the office? How easy is it to get to? What's the lighting like? Where can they have lunch?

For young businesses, a few desks in a relatively central location might be all they're looking for, but there is so much more to think about to attract top talent, especially as you grow. You've got to ask yourself the right questions, and a lot of those are around the physical infrastructure you have in place.

It's no different if you *are* that top talent. Forget about the package and the job title for a minute. It's easy to snap up a new role because it's a promotion and better paid. But have you envisaged what it'll be like actually working for your new company?

In almost every interview, at some point, the interviewer will ask, "Have you got any questions for us?" It's an incredibly awkward moment when you don't have anything prepared, so, no doubt, you know this and have rehearsed a few that will make you sound both passionate about the company and up to date on the industry. But seldom do people talk about what really matters: What's it like to work there?

"Any questions for us?" Jeff says, leaning back in his chair as if he's already clocking off.

"Ah, I'm glad you asked," you say. "I just want to get a feel for what the day to day will be like. I've written a list, if you don't mind me sharing it?"

Jeff looks pleasantly surprised. "No, no, by all

means, Stuart, thanks for coming so prepared," he replies. For the first time, he acknowledges his assistant, who's been taking notes throughout the interview. "Tommy here will jot everything down and come back to you, but we'll answer what we can here and now. What's on your mind?"

You reach into your bag, pull out your iPad and select your notes.

"First of all," you say. "Is this your private office, because it looks fantastic?"

"Ah, thank you. Yes, well, I spend a lot of time in this room, so I've put a lot of thought into it."

"What's your favourite bit?"

"Oh, definitely the fridge. It's also a TV, look!" He presses the remote, and the front of the fridge lights up for a second before displaying Sky Sports in perfect 4K clarity.

"Wow, no expense spared," you say. "I'd love to have a look around the rest of the office if there's time? I'm sure you've sprinkled a little magic everywhere."

"Sure, yeah," Jeff says, suddenly unable to take his eyes off the football. "We can show you on the way out. What else were you thinking?"

"You know, just functional stuff mainly. Let me see here: Are we on fixed desks, or is there an element of hot desking? How much time do people spend working from home? How do you find that affects the office dynamic? Where do we sit when we're not at our desks?"

Tommy leans forward. "Er, sorry," he says, finally looking up from his keyboard. "How do you mean, 'When you're not at your desks?'"

"Well, is there a communal area for lunch, or do we eat at our computers? Is there somewhere we can unwind over a book or a game of pool? Where do people chat?"

Jeff barks out a laugh, but when he realises you're serious, he reins himself in. "Ah, yes," he says, clearing his throat. "That's a good point. There's a small area with a sofa, but we are looking into a more communal space. Not a lot of time for unwinding, though; we're all GO GO GO."

You nod your head. "Yeah, I can, erm, I can see that," you say, checking your list. "Just another few things then, really." You turn around and look through the glass door. "I didn't notice any meeting rooms. Where's the nearest coffee shop? Is that good for a face to face with the team?"

"Well, there is one about a 10-minute walk away, I think," Jeff says.

"What's it like?" you say.

"In what way?" Tommy replies.

"Well, is it quiet? Comfy? Could you take a client there? At the very least, is the coffee drinkable?"

"We haven't actually been there," Jeff says.

"Yeah, I'll have to get back to you on that," Tommy adds.

"Okay, how about shops?" you say. "Where do people go for lunch?"

"Packed lunches mostly," Jeff says.

"Cool," you say. "That should save me some pennies, at least. Is there an oven or a microwave in the kitchen?"

"Well, it's... it's more of a kitchenette, really," Jeff says. "But yes, there's a microwave."

"We also have a kettle and a dishwasher," Tommy adds.

You squint slightly to focus on the far end of the office. "Great, great. Oh, I see it. Is there a fridge behind one of the cupboards, then?"

"A fridge! Yes, that's a great idea," Jeff says, nodding to Tommy, who taps away on his laptop. "We'll, er, have to look into that. No one wants a warm sandwich, do they?"

By this point, you've seen more red flags than the Moroccan Olympic team, but you just can't help yourself. "How do most people get here then? It took me 40 minutes to walk from the station. And I didn't spot much parking on the way in."

"Ah, I'm glad you mentioned that," Tommy says, clearly excited to be so involved. "We've just signed up for the Cycle to Work Scheme, actually."

"Oh, brilliant. I bet it was a pain getting all the bike racks installed."

Tommy's eyes light up like he's been caught shoplifting. "Bike racks!" he says. "Yes, bike racks, we're actually working on that too."

"Of course we are," Jeff says. "It wouldn't do to have 30 bikes stacked up in the hallway now, would it?"

Tommy's sycophantic laugh sends a shiver down your spine.

"No, of course not," you reply. "Unless you want the place looking like a collision at the Tour de France. What about showers?"

"Showers?" Jeff says. "Well, we suggest one before coming to work, but some people like them the night before, don't they?" He looks at Tommy for support who nods along.

"Er, no, sorry," you say, shaking your head clear. "I meant, are there showers here? If 30 people are cycling in over the summer, you're either going to need some showers or a pretty hefty incense budget."

As you laugh, you notice Tommy slyly removing a pack of incense from the desk and lowering it onto his lap.

You've had enough. "Speaking of sweat," you say, "how do you handle a heatwave? Is there any air-con? What about heaters for the chilly winters?" You stand up and walk over to the window, pointing at the nearest row of desks. "Also, those chairs seem more like something you'd find in a school assembly hall. Can people really sit in those for eight hours? Look at her, she's clutching her lower back. In fact, do you reckon I could have a quick chat with the team? I'd love to see how they feel about—"

"That'll be all, thank you, Stuart," Jeff snaps. "You've done remarkably well, but we really must be getting on." He stands up and strides towards you, holding out his hand. "Tommy here will be in touch to answer the rest of your questions, and we'll let you know about a potential start day. Thanks for coming in."

"No problem," you say, grasping Jeff's hand firmly. "Any chance of a lift back to the station?"

* * *

As a business owner, there's some basic infrastructure that you must think about before signing up for an office. Just because it's close to your house and has soft furnishings in the lobby doesn't mean it's right for everyone. You've got to visualise the day to day. Close your eyes and picture being an employee. What's their journey like? Where are they sitting? How much light do they get? How far's the toilet? Where can they go for beers after work? Is there a local gym?

You may be thinking, *Whatever we end up with, if I can handle it, so can the staff. I'm not asking them to do anything I wouldn't do.*

Well, maybe you're right. Some people will follow your example, but you won't attract top talent, and if you do, keeping them will be another matter entirely. A 21 year old in their first job who doesn't know any better might be happy just to be there. But people who have been employed in top businesses won't be used to losing three quarters of their lunch break every day just to find somewhere to buy a sandwich. They'll care about how rough the area is when they leave at night and how bad the chairs are for their backs.

Perhaps you don't need to be in town, or you'd like a bigger place with cheaper rent and a warehouse out the back. There's nothing wrong with that, but how are the staff going to get to you? Have you decided who you're giving company cars to? How big's the car park? What about if clients come to visit? Have you worked out what happens when they arrive? Do you sign them in? Is there a waiting area? What about tea and biscuits? Is that the receptionist's job? Do you even have a receptionist? Maybe there's a coffee machine; who's paying for the drinks, the business or the client? What about if it's raining? Do you give out umbrellas to people who need them?

You can't think of everything, but everything you

do think of, write it down. Get into the habit of creating processes to look back on. You'll thank yourself five years from now.

RULE OF THUMB

Shop for
the future.

You've signed a 10-year lease on a forecourt where you can work on your vehicles. You've done the math and the site has enough electricity to sustain the number of cars you're servicing. You've checked the water, sewage and gas. There's even a little office for the five of you to work from.

Great! You've solved your immediate problems. Now, what happens if your business does well? Suddenly, you've got three people sharing one desk, cars unable to book for weeks at a time, and too many parts to fit in the warehouse.

Ask yourself, if your business hits (or exceeds) your quarterly targets, will you be forced to move again soon? If the answer is 'yes' or 'maybe', then why did you sign a 10-year lease? And what about the office? How are you going to squeeze everyone in now your company has doubled in size? Even if you can, will there be enough rest rooms, parking spaces or bandwidth?

As a business owner, you've got to be able to think things through, and the more you can visualise the minor details, the better you'll be at controlling the bigger picture.

Online Infrastructure

One morning, a newspaper on Fleet Street has 680 employees; a week later, they move to the Docklands, having downsized to 68 staff. That's technology.

When new software comes into your organisation, it can be a massive advantage. You're always looking at ways to reduce labour costs and increase productivity, so anything that speeds up your processes and requires fewer people is worth considering. A lot of founders are resistant to change, though, thinking that what got them to a certain size or turnover is the only thing that will propel them forward. My view is that you *have* to evolve, you must keep learning and use that learning wisely.

I've always welcomed anything that provides the intel we need to help us run our businesses right, so when I first came across software that gave us access to live information, it left me wondering how we'd ever got this far without it. Our new systems allowed us to view management accounts at the click of a button, monitor real-time ticket sales, and manage stock with pinpoint accuracy. It's no exaggeration to say that when our stock levels were itemised, it *revolutionised* City Cruises. We now knew every single product that was sold, at any time of day, and in which direction the boats were travelling at the time. Knowing the what, where and when meant we could start figuring out the why.

RULE OF THUMB

Don't guess.

Perhaps you have five types of beer on tap. Why can't you sell four? Would it damage your income or your reputation if you sold one less, or would it make it easier for the team behind the bar? What about storage? Would it free up some space in the cellar? Would it give you more room behind the bar? Which beer are you going to lose, though? What's got the biggest margin? Which one sells the most? Which one sells the least? How much cash do you have tied up in stock? If you know February's a quiet month, why not buy less? But how much less?

You can't make these kinds of decisions if you don't have enough information, and with the number of tools available to you online these days, the only thing stopping you is your own initiative. Ask yourself: What information am I tracking? Where am I storing it? How do I retrieve that information, and how do I allow the right people to access it in an instant?

For most of us, labour costs are going to be the biggest expense to our companies (there's a reason HR and staffing have been a major focus of this book). As such, we need to be especially meticulous about things like recruitment, wage reviews, payroll and balancing the rota, because if you make too many mistakes here, it could quite easily clean you out.

* * *

Dominic owns a pop-up immersive experience. It's hugely popular, and people have been clamouring for tickets every time a new run is announced. The problem is he's always struggled with his staffing levels. The only time they get negative feedback is when there just aren't enough hands on deck. Last weekend was a case in point. Everything went wrong; people spent ages queuing outside the venue in the cold, it took well over half an hour to get served at the bar, the tables were cluttered with empty plates and glasses, and the toilets looked like something out of *Trainspotting*. Unsurprisingly, a slew of bad reviews ended up on Google:

⭐ "Worst night ever."

⭐ "I WANT MY MONEY BACK!"

⭐⭐ "I've had better service on Ben Nevis."

⭐⭐ "If those toilets could talk, they'd press charges."

Now, in Dominic's defence, if everyone had simply showed up to work, they might have been okay. All it took was a couple of people phoning in sick and a particularly rowdy crowd that night, and everything fell apart. He knows he needs to make up for it next weekend, so maybe he just sticks one more person on the door, one more on the bar and one more cleaning the tables. If he's read some of this book, he might even decide to have an extra person on the rota just in case someone phones in sick. Will that fix the problem, though? It's not enough to know how many extra staff he needs; he has to know his budget. Can he afford to put an extra four people on? Or, by this point, should he just cancel the show? It's a big call, but he can't throw good money after bad. If the event is losing him money, why is he doing it?

So, what can Dominic do? Well, if he has the right information, he can be more tactical. When does he need the extra people? Just at the weekends? For all the evening performances? Only on Saturdays? Between what times is the bar at its busiest? Does he even have enough space behind the bar if he adds another person? Why are people queuing outside? Is the coat check-in too slow?

The less Dominic knows, the harder it is for him to solve these problems. Thankfully, he's been implementing processes all the way along. He's realised that one person is phoning in sick every week. To combat that, he's marked on the rota an extra person for evening shifts. If everyone comes in as planned, he has an extra set of hands in the coat check-in for an hour and then clearing tables in the evening. If the night quietens down, he can then send someone home early.

It turns out he doesn't have enough room behind the bar for more people, so he's had to think outside the box. On the busier nights, he schedules two extra staff between 6pm and 9pm to do table service. This reduces the number of people queuing at the bar, opens up more space in the venue and makes customers feel much more looked after. He budgets for everything accordingly and allows for a drop in profit. It must have been a nice moment when he figured out that this approach actually made him *more* money!

His staff now have the time and capacity to upsell to the customers. They can walk around the venue and spot when a group have nearly finished their drinks. The servers can then nip over, see if everything is okay and offer them another round. By the time the last remnants of their cocktails are being slurped through their paper straws, their replacements are already on the table.

Dominic studied live spending over the next few weeks and decided to introduce table service to all of the shows. With the help of reliable data, he turned a financial headache into a profitable solution.

RULE OF THUMB

The stronger the information, the better the decisions.

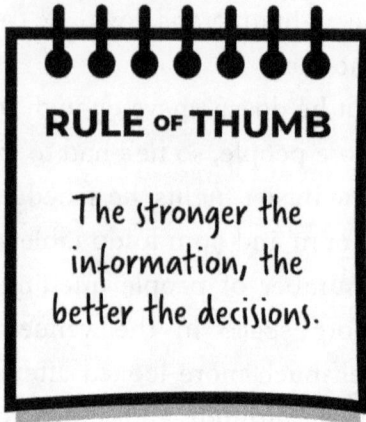

When people first step into business for themselves, it doesn't take long for the old adage "Cash Flow is King" to rear its head. Cash flow is integral for any business, but especially for a young company with minimal lines of credit. Why, then, for example, do so many small businesses buy far too much stock? The answer is often the obvious one: they have no idea how much they need. When you first start out, that's forgivable, but as you grow, you have days', weeks, or months' worth of previous orders at your fingertips, you must learn how to use them.

Thanks to our software, we could easily monitor when we were getting low on certain products, receive alerts, and prepare for the weeks ahead. It helped us to restock long before we ran out of anything, and with the help of actual facts, we could negotiate better deals with our suppliers and avoid committing to any unreachable targets. Technology has helped to make business a science. With the right data, you can try new things, iterate based on facts, test what worked, and figure out why things are failing. Once you have drawn your conclusions, you can then factor them into sound decision making.

In the '90s, we launched a product called Show Boat, a pleasure craft that would take passengers on a night out up the River Thames, with live music, dinner and dancing. While it was hugely popular, there was a problem with the business model. The vessel was out hosting parties every evening and then sat around doing nothing all day (it was like having another teenager to look after!). We noticed that what was an asset to us at night became a liability just 12 hours later. Our mindset became: *If it's empty, it's costing us money.*

We decided to trial a lunchtime cruise. Whilst it didn't take off right away, we had the patience to test out different menus, figure out what people wanted most and give it to them. Once we'd built up that product, we still had a big gap until the evening performances, so we picked another English staple – cream tea – and sent the boat out again mid-afternoon. From one trip a day, we were now out for lunch, tea *and* dinner. One seat on the boat could now generate £40 for lunch, £40 for tea, and £100 for dinner. For a 100-capacity boat, that's an extra £8,000 per day.

Very quickly, Show Boat turned into a two-million-pound per year product, and we hired more staff and full-time chefs to cope with the demand. And this was just one of what became a fleet of over 40 vessels. To operate on this scale (and to get there in the first place), we had to track everything, understand the data, and learn how to use it.

Just the Ticket

The evolution of our ticket machines is a great example of how leaning into technology can revolutionise a business. We used to print out little yellow tickets that looked more like you were entering a raffle than going on a sightseeing journey. We decided we wanted to present a proper brand to our customers, give them more information about their trip, and maybe even something they could keep as a souvenir.

We upgraded to a huge touchscreen device that printed on larger paper. This meant the ticket could now house meaningful information, such as the time, date, cost and destination. After all that, there was still space to advertise other services *and* give our logo pride of place.

The problem then became office space. You may be old enough to remember how chunky phones were at the turn of the century – it was like holding a loaf of bread to your head every time you wanted to make a call. Our touchscreens were huge, which wasn't ideal on the South Bank, where space was at a premium.

A few years later, the technology (and its affordability) had moved along, so we switched to computers. We could now fit two screens – with two people selling behind them – within the footprint of one old machine. This all seems like a no-brainer now, of course, but when we started, people didn't use computers and we had no email or internet. All of a sudden, the world sped up. We could build a database of clients *online* and people could access it anytime, from anywhere in the world. Mobile phones came in and helped us to communicate with our fleet. Card payments reduced the risk of theft. Everything was changing.

People eventually stopped buying physical tickets. Instead of our staff running through London with Del Boy's back catalogue of French phrases and a briefcase full of tickets, customers became conditioned to do it all themselves. They saw the social media posts, went to the website, found a slot, made a purchase, paid for their ticket and even downloaded it themselves. A CEO could wake up, jump on an app and see they'd sold 350 tickets whilst sleeping. Life's become one giant self-checkout.

Printing is a great example of how technology changes a market. Print used to be one of the largest costs for businesses. Going to a meeting? Print a map. Heading to a sales pitch? Print out your proposal, and don't forget one for each person in the boardroom. Got a report to review? Grab your highlighter and print it out. That report then needed to be *physically* handed to some other poor sap who then had the enjoyable task of deciphering your handwriting. Contrast that to now. No faxing, minimal scanning. You jump on Google Docs and write suggestions in the comments – and then you're done. You can even work on it at the same time as other people.

Imagine if I saw you at a networking event and tried to give you a brochure of my company's services. You'd either smile and say, "No thanks", or take it out of politeness and pop it straight in the next bin. If you want to keep up to date with us now, you can follow us on social media within 10 seconds; all you have to do is grab your phone out of your pocket. Physical brochures may have once been a necessity, but they were never actually that practical. Things change all the time in business: menus, capacities, prices, legislation, health and safety and special offers, and you need to be able to change alongside them.

RULE OF THUMB

Either you innovate or the market does it for you.

Take poor Jimmy, for instance. He waits in line at Kall Kwik for an hour until his sales pamphlets are printed. When they're finished, he grabs the two boxes and hops in a cab to take them back to the office. On the way, he gets an email from his boss. "Due to the ongoing concerns made by the surveyor, we've taken the three flats on Hampton Street off the market for the foreseeable."

Jimmy looks down at his glossy, 10-page brochure. Three of those pages are already out of date, and he hasn't even put his seatbelt on yet. Should he go back and print more? Can he just rip the pages out? Maybe he can just tell every client that those ones are no longer available. But what if they ask why? Should he be honest?

The answer doesn't really matter here, what matters is that it's a pain in the backside. Being able to hop online and remove those flats from a PDF or a website saves time, money and many embarrassing conversations.

Processes

Derrick has invented a drill with a diamond tip that will go through anything. It's such a unique and useful product that he hopes he can start a company and, one day, make enough money to quit his day job. But almost as soon as he puts the wheels in motion, he's hit with the reality of how many processes there are before he can even get his product to market.

For a while, he's been focusing on finding a way to produce the drills in bulk, but this means sourcing more raw materials, and to do that, he needs to find some money. He has no idea where to start, though; should he get a loan, seek investment, or dip into his life savings?

As he weighs up his options, he decides to take a few steps back. He needs something to demonstrate to the stakeholders he's in talks with. He can't just turn up to meetings, pull a drill out of its holster, spin it around a few times and blow on the end like a cowboy with a side hustle. If people are going to take Derrick's drill seriously, he needs to think about his brand and maybe work on a logo and a company website.

One afternoon, he bumps into his friend, Kathy, who owns a local grocery store, and she agrees to join him for a quick coffee to discuss the venture. Before Derrick's even had his first sip, he wishes he hadn't asked.

"So, how are you going to market the drill, then? What's the plan?" Kathy asks. "And more importantly, *who* are you marketing it to? Have you spoken to any potential customers yet?"

Derrick looks down nervously. He's about to reply, but Kathy is on a mission.

"I'll take that as a no," she says. "You need to find out their reaction to it. Does it solve any problems for them? If you're hoping for investment, you have to understand the current marketplace. And you better start working on your figures."

Derrick instinctively places a hand over his pot belly.

"Not your *figure*, darling. Your figures!" she says behind a cackle. "How much do you need? What are your overheads? What kind of return can they expect?"

Return? Derrick thinks. He glances around the café, hoping his chair will swallow him up. *I don't even have a company name yet and she thinks I'm Lord Alan Sugar.*

As his mind wanders in and out of the conversation, he hears words like *invoicing, payment terms, bank account and VAT*, and he begins to nod along like a man receiving tragic news.

"What about the packaging and distribution?" she says as he tunes back in. "What's it going to look like in the stores? Have you got any examples?"

Derrick looks back at his coffee and swirls it in his mug. "I mean, I have ideas," he says. "They're just, ya know" – he taps himself on the temple – "in here at the moment."

Kathy scrunches up her lips. "You haven't written anything down, have you?"

Derrick shakes his head.

"If you don't write it down, it doesn't exist," she says.

Kathy dives into her handbag and pulls out a pen and a notebook. She flicks through to a blank page, writes the date in the top corner and looks up with a smile. "Right!" she says, "let's start with an easy one. What's your company called?"

Derrick gulps.

The next morning, Derrick's head is still spinning with information, but he's determined to get his ideas down on paper. He comes up with a dozen company names and a few rough logos. He contacts a handful of freelancers on Fiver and asks them to send him a quote for a landing page. Bit by bit, he chips away at dozens of tasks he never knew existed.

One afternoon, while fixing a diamond onto the end of his latest drill, he realises he has nowhere near enough space to do this in bulk, and it's becoming far too costly and time-consuming to do in such small quantities. Before he can manufacture anything, though, he needs to find premises. But that leads to another set of problems. If he has a warehouse, he'll need more staff, as well as some basic infrastructure like internet, lighting, heating and storage. Within a couple of months, he's gone from making drills for fun to being asked to sign lengthy leases and personal guarantees. He's starting to wonder what he's let himself in for.

Derrick creates a spreadsheet of all the property agents he's speaking to. On the notes application on his phone, he tracks all his meetings and communications until they read like a step-by-step guide to leasing a property.

As he perseveres, he slowly figures out each area of his business, eventually managing to get his product online and generate a small income. Thanks to a bank loan and a modest turnover, he's able to quit his day job and focus on the business full-time.

He hires a new employee with a fantastic sales background who quickly gets the drill on the shelves of some local stores. Within a few more months, Derrick's able to recruit a part-time finance person to take over the invoicing.

With each role that's filled, he can feel the weight on his shoulders begin to lighten. In two years, he goes from a one-man band to a fully-fledged business with sales and marketing, distribution and finance departments. Derrick can finally focus more on what he loves – improving the product.

The problem is, somewhere along the way, Derrick stopped writing things down. Once again, everything is in his head. Not only that, he's built a company culture where no one else writes anything down either, and sooner or later, it's going to come back and bite him.

As sales continue to pick up, Fred takes over warehouse operations. He's been hired to put together a team to help manufacture more drills and work on a strategy to speed up delivery. He's a fast learner and manages to improve logistics right away, making sweeping changes that increase efficiency, propelling them into the realms of a more grown-up business.

Meanwhile, Derrick is very happy, patting himself on the back for another great hire. He's a fan of people who go out and get things done, and if it's working, there's no need for him to interfere. Then, one morning, Fred has an accident. He falls off his motorbike on a weekend trip in the Cotswolds and spends a month convalescing in hospital.

At first, the warehouse ticks over just fine. The current orders are already set to go out, and only a handful reach the customers late. Then it all starts to fall apart.

Fred's assistant is a young lad named Connor. Connor has a problem. He has 150 orders to fulfil but no idea how to organise the deliveries efficiently. He knows he has to inform some of the customers that their goods will be late again, but he doesn't have access to the spreadsheet with their contact details.

Derrick is enjoying a fry-up with his wife when his phone rings. He thinks about not answering it for a second, but when he sees it's from the warehouse, he gives a deep sigh and picks up the call.

"Hello," Derrick says, a little more sternly than he meant.

"Oh, hi. Sorry, Derrick. It's Connor from the warehouse. I... erm... I haven't... well, you better come down here, actually."

Derrick's stomach drops. "Is everyone okay?"

"Yeah, sorry, no one's hurt. It's just, I don't... well, I hate to say this, but I have no idea what I'm doing."

Derrick rolls his eyes. Doing his best not to let Connor know he's still chewing on a sausage, he says,

"Okay... don't worry; I'll be right down. Just get everything together, and I'll help you figure it out."

"Thanks, Derrick, I really—"

Derrick puts down the phone and turns to his wife. "He's been here six months, that kid. Surely it can't be that hard," he says.

"Don't worry," she replies with a comforting smile. "You've done Fred's job longer than he has; I'm sure you'll be in and out of there."

Derrick finally swallows his mouthful of food and makes a sign for the bill. He's lost his appetite.

Within 10 minutes of being in the warehouse, Derrick is starting to panic. Everything's different. He hired Fred to streamline his processes, and to his credit, he's done exactly that. The problem is that these "processes" are all in his head – and Fred's *head* is in a hospital bed.

Derrick is looking through the few files that Connor has been able to scrape together. An invoice, a couple of phone numbers with no context, and some scribbles that might as well be hieroglyphics.

"Is this it?" he says, trying to rein in his fury. "Where do you keep the orders?"

Connor blinks. "Erm, I dunno. Fred just tells me."

"Okay. What time do the deliveries usually go out?"

Connor looks at his watch. "Hard to saaaay, really. Sometimes th—"

"Okay, how about an easy one. What's the new company called again, the one that provides the lorries and the drivers?"

"Oh..." Connor squeezes his eyes shut as he thinks.

Derrick taps his foot impatiently. He's just about to say something when Connor's eyelids burst open. "Prime Haulage?" he shouts, excited that he's got one right.

Derrick lifts his thumbs. "O...kay, great," he says. "Well done. Who are we dealing with over there? Can you grab me their phone number, please?"

"Oh, yeah, er... it's... hang on, one sec."

Connor zooms across the warehouse and Derrick is left staring into the abyss. For a moment, he wonders if Connor is ever coming back. Then it hits him. Nothing has been documented. There are no contact lists, instructions, or even order forms. And even if there are, there's nothing to say where these files are located or how to access them. There's clearly been no training down here, and poor Connor's probably been used for nothing more than coffee runs and heavy lifting.

Derrick catches his jaded reflection in the window. *This might be my fault,* he thinks.

He remembers his first meeting with Kathy; what was it she said to him? He pulls his phone out of his pocket and flicks over to his notes tab. *I'm sure I wrote it down*, he thinks. Near the top of the list is an entry entitled OFFICE LEASE. It was dated two years ago. As he scrolls through the text, he recognises that it would be a huge help if he ever needs another site. It has everything: the names of who he spoke to, the places he saw, the Ts and Cs he wasn't sure about, the average cost per square foot in the area, all the suppliers he used along the way.

That reminds me, he thinks, *I need to change energy supplier.*

The sound of someone knocking over a dozen drill bits rattles against the warehouse walls, and Derrick is shaken from his thoughts. A shadow appears beside him.

"I couldn't find the name," Connor says between heavy breaths, "but I got a phone number for reception."

Derrick smiles. "Don't worry about that for now, Connor. Grab your coat and meet me upstairs in five minutes. You and I are going to talk to every person in this building today."

"Er, okay!" Connor says as he edges towards the staff room.

"Oh, and Connor," Derrick shouts.

"Yeah?"

"Bring a pen."

RULE OF THUMB

If you don't
write it down,
it doesn't exist.

Every department should have its own processes. Even something as simple as a salesperson receiving a signed contract from a client. Who checks the deal to make sure the numbers are correct? Who countersigns the contract and sends it back to the client? Who creates the invoice? How quickly is that invoice sent? Who chases the deposit payment? When is the client expecting delivery? Is there a referral scheme in place?

These things are second nature to the founder of the business, who's been working in the role for 18 months. But you can't just 'tell someone who tells someone' and hope that nobody misses anything. Every member of the team should be trained in these processes, and crucially, they must be written down.

Whether an employee storms out in a fury, phones in sick, has an accident, quits or gets fired, it's all the same problem. There must be a process that somebody else can step in and follow in their absence.

It's not just about efficiency either, sometimes it's quite literally a matter of life and death. We touch on health and safety later in this chapter, but the processes you put in place are a huge component for the protection of your staff, customers, contractors, suppliers and even your liberty.

Corporate manslaughter is one of the scariest terms for anyone in business. God forbid somebody is injured or dies as a result of your operation. But if that day does come, and you appear in court, you must be able to stand there and answer questions honestly.

When they ask, "Have you trained your staff?" what is your response?

"Yeah, I sit with them whenever they have questions and go over everything" isn't going to cut it. Do you factor in new laws and legislation? Is the training consistently refreshed? How do people access this information when the training ends? Who hosts the training? Are they qualified in the areas they're teaching? What processes are in place to stop accidents like this happening? What processes failed on this occasion?

You need receipts. If you can share printouts of all your procedures clearly documented from day one, not only are you protecting yourself and your business, you're much less likely to be in court in the first place.

More Than Just a Suggestion

There's a well-known story from the early 20th century about an employee at Swan Vesta, the match manufacturer. Whilst working on the production line, he noticed an area of the business that could be more cost-efficient. Rather than keep it to himself, he approached his bosses with what he told them was "a million-dollar idea." At first, he struggled to get an audience with the board; he was just a lowly factory worker after all, but after months of persistence, he'd finally made enough noise to get himself in the room. When he was there, it didn't take much: one sentence changed everything.

"So, why do we have the sandpaper strike on both sides of our matchboxes?"

I like to imagine what the people in that room must have been thinking as the implications of this crescendoed around the table.

"How do you mean?"

"Well, we only need it on one side, don't we?"

"That's a good point! Why *is* it on both sides?"

Pandemonium. Everyone talks at once. People are throwing paper up in the air, running in and out of the room, routing through old documents and draws, emptying out cupboards, grabbing their colleagues like Homer strangling Bart, hoping to shake hard enough that the answer falls out of their ears. All the while, our hero just leans against the wall with his arms folded watching the chaos ensue.

I have no idea how much money they saved, but a "million-dollar" idea is likely vastly underselling it.

RULE OF THUMB

Talk to your
employees.

The staff at the coal face will know how to get coal out of a mine better than anyone else. They're down there all day, every day, year after year. You need to talk to them.

What does a coal miner want? I imagine it's not groundbreaking stuff (ironically). Like anyone, they want to get home safe, clean and knowing they've done a great job. They want to be paid in full and on time, and they don't want to go hungry or thirsty.

Then there are the specifics: Where do they get their lunch from? How do they eat it? Do they have disposable forks, or are they eating it with grubby hands? What are they drinking? Is there a water fountain back in the office? How far is that from where they actually work? Where do they go to the toilet?

What you're looking for is ways you can make their lives better. Could you build a canteen that gives your staff somewhere to congregate at break times, clean up, relieve themselves, and head back into the mine with their energy meter fully restored?

Is the lighting giving them headaches? Or maybe they can barely see a thing down there. How's their posture when in confined spaces? Could you pay for a masseuse to come and visit once a week.

If you're not careful, you might not even find out what's bothering people until it's too late; perhaps the performance levels drop, or your best workers hand in their notice around the same time. Even if you are in dialogue with them, there are still things that some people just won't want to say to their boss.

But the good news is that with just one tiny

addition to your front desk, you can reap massive rewards. In around 1770, the British Navy implemented a Suggestion Box to gather ideas from their sailors by giving them a place to provide anonymous feedback. The idea may have been taken from the eighth shogun of Japan, who, as early as 1721, placed a box outside a castle for his subjects to leave their thoughts. They hit the mainstream in the West when the Allies used them in the Second World War, with the US making propaganda films about plant workers who submitted suggestions that increased efficiency and the economy.

This minor innovation will allow your staff to feel like they're being heard, offers the choice of anonymity and means you can shake new ideas out of a hive mind that's plugged into what you do every day. Just make sure you reward the best ideas appropriately, and if you're implementing them, bring the suggester on the journey with you.

Whatever happens, I can promise you this: There will be more innovative ideas coming from your suggestion box than from most chairpersons you're ever likely to work with. I say "most" because when I was last a chairman, I actually had an incredible idea that helped transform the business. "Let's get a suggestion box," I said.

Health & Safety

If you're fortunate enough to last a few decades in business, you'll have to deal with all kinds of stresses along the way. Some you can shrug off as experience, others you might need to wash away with a pint (or three) and a good friend, but there will always be those that stick with you forever.

When you own a company, you're looking to serve your customers. Especially in hospitality. Sure, you want to make some money, buy a house and set your family up for a cushy life, but first and foremost, you just want to entertain people.

When you start out, the last thing you're thinking is that any of your employees, suppliers or customers might get hurt. We're all busy imagining creating something so wonderful that everyone is singing its praises, writing us emails about how great the experience is, and how they were so inspired by the magic of the event that they proposed to their partner at the end of the night!

But what happens if the phone call you receive one evening is that your customer never made it home. Maybe they fell over and hit their head, or took too many drugs and overdosed in your restrooms, or had a heart attack while navigating the stairs.

You have to sleep at night knowing you did

everything you could to keep your people safe. There are many advantages that come with being your own boss, but this is definitely where the fun stops.

So, when I see young business owners rolling their eyes at filling out risk assessments, I know they haven't been around the block. Give it a few years, and I'm sure the value of it will start to sink in, hopefully before it's too late.

Yes, health and safety might seem to have gone mad in recent years, but if you look at it objectively, it actually hasn't gone far enough. If people are still dying at work, or customers are getting seriously hurt on a night out with friends, something must be done about it. People will argue that "Accidents happen", "You can't account for bad luck", or "You can follow all the rules, and people can still get hurt."

All those things can be true, but as business *owners*, we need to do just that: take *ownership*. We need to make sure we're working with experts in their field, constantly training our staff, and having the processes in place that not only reduce risk but also mitigate our liability.

If you're not careful, one accident – a customer falling over a step, an employee crashing a company vehicle – and you could be facing thousands of pounds in lawsuits. In more severe cases, bankruptcy, criminal prosecution, and perhaps the most harrowing – the knowledge that you could have done more.

Assess the Risk

You've got to read the legislation and understand what applies to you and your industry (being part of a trade organisation will help you with this). Then you need to do a risk assessment, but you can't just wing it. You must have someone who understands them, someone who cares about not having incidents on their watch, perhaps someone whose reputation is tied up in the outcome. Hire an independent professional or outsource it to a company that specialises in them.

If a "freak accident" does occur, you need to be able to point to all the things you did along the way because, quite rightly, everything will be scrutinised. Next, you need to train your staff and *keep* training them. If your event evolves or you notice certain things, update your risk assessment and add it to your training.

Let's use a very common example: A trip hazard like a step.

Your customer came to your venue and had a great time. When they left, they walked outside, tripped over the step and broke their wrist. The next morning, you get a scathing letter from her telling you to "Lawyer up, buddy."

Who's at fault?

You check the CCTV. Just before she left, she was slamming tequilas like there was no tomorrow, giggling all the way down the corridor and looking at her phone when she stepped onto the street.

If your defence is that she can't handle her drink, it's unlikely to hold up. By law, you're not allowed to sell alcohol to someone who is intoxicated. Now, where the line is between casual drinking and intoxication is something you'll have to figure out. But what matters here is that if she was drunk *before* necking that tequila and you sold her more, that argument is not going to help your case.

If you know there's a step, and it's a hazard, tell people. On your email communications make it clear: *Please mind the step on the way in and out of the venue.* Put a sign up on the door. Have a staff member or the bouncer reminding people as they pass through.

As you say, accidents may still happen, but when you get a call from a law firm, or you're in court the following year, what would you rather say?

"We tell people about the step on the way in," or, "We sent an email out warning customers about the step, we have a sign on both sides of the door, we had a dedicated person helping people out, and we painted the step white with a yellow arrow on the pavement pointing at it. Plus, we put a light on it and a railing."

Now, you might *still* lose the case, but all you can do is prepare yourself. Heaven forbid someone tripped and broke their neck; what could you tell yourself in bed at night? *I should have trained the staff better? I should have been stricter? I knew that step was a problem; I should have just asked the door person to add it to their list of duties?*

Put it in the job description. You can't blame the manager because, ultimately, the buck stops with you. That's *your* manager. Why weren't they trained? You started a business and as a result, somebody came to your venue with great expectations and didn't make it home in one piece.

When Enough is Never Enough

We had a claim once from a lady who never even made it to us. She got out of the taxi down the road from our venue, and as she shut the door, she fell over and broke her arm. The taxi driver helped her up, popped her back in the cab, and drove her to St Thomas' Hospital. The first we knew about it was receiving a claim. We lost that case.

So, the question becomes: When is the customer a customer?

Let's say Tommy bought a ticket to see his

favourite band at the O2 in London. He lives in Birmingham, so getting the train home after the show will be a bit of a pain. Instead, he checks into a local hotel for two nights. The gig's not until the Saturday, but Tommy doesn't want to risk any train issues spoiling his party, so he takes the day off work and heads down a day early. On Friday evening, he wraps up a day of sightseeing by heading to a nice restaurant with his wife. When he gets there, he sits down and opens Instagram. He looks up at his wife in horror and says, "They've cancelled the concert."

As the promoter, at what point is Tommy your customer? When he leaves the house? When he arrives at the venue? Or from the moment he buys a ticket?

This highlights the importance of having robust Ts and Cs. If you promote a show and the singer gets so sick they can't take the stage, people are likely to come at you for more than just their ticket value. Are you liable for Tommy's travel? What about his hotel? Or his day off work?

You may think that all you do is deal with them when they arrive, but if they purchase tickets to go to your venue, they have to get there. What if the show finishes at 1am? How do they get home? What if there are train strikes? What's the alternative route? Did you write to them before they arrived and say, "Thank you for purchasing your tickets. Here's how you can get to the venue. As the show finishes late, please check your trains are still running. Here's a list of local hotels. Please do not arrive intoxicated."

RULE OF THUMB

Every part of your customers' journey is your problem.

You can't account for every scenario, but you can mitigate your risk. If you promote a concert and the venue has to cancel your event because of a security alert, who pays for that? What do their Ts and Cs say? What do yours say? Do you have Ts and Cs? And if so, be honest: have you just copied and pasted someone else's and changed the names to your business?

There is a cost to having a professional look them over, sure, but remember, there is a much bigger cost on the horizon if you don't.

Chapter 3

Managing Money

Budgets

How much are you going to spend this year? How much will you make? It's almost impossible to know this down to the penny, but as we progress in business, we're looking to collect enough information so that one day, our predictions feel more like premonitions.

Let's start with the basics. Much like your personal life, you have fixed and variable costs. At home, you probably know exactly how much rent you'll pay each month, but your coffee and bagel costs might fluctuate depending on how the diet goes from one week to the next. In the early days of tracking your finances, it can feel like you're standing on a sand dune with your finger in the air trying to figure out the direction of the wind. At first, no matter how many times you lick your finger, you still get a face full of sand.

The bad news is that unexpected costs are going to keep popping up. The good news is that the more information you collect, especially in the first few years, the less they'll have an impact. The trick is to keep tracking your progress and adjust your budget accordingly. Then one day, you'll have enough pieces of the puzzle to see the bigger picture.

RULE of THUMB

Every company
needs a budget.

So, what are the fixed costs for your business? Here are some things to look out for: rent, rates, electrics, gas, insurance, bank charges, accountants, staff, hardware, software and your salary. Then there are your variable costs, such as stock, commissions, freelancer fees, shipping costs, maintenance and repairs.

What you're searching for is a number that represents your break-even point; in other words, how much do I need to make to start turning a profit? From here, you can set your aspirational targets and work towards increasing your margins.

In 2022, Fundsquire, a global start-up funding network, reported that 20% of small businesses in the UK fail in their first year, and approximately 60% fail within the first three. The level of information you keep today may be the difference between outlasting almost half your peers or winding down the company before you've ever *really* got going.

The Subtle Art of Not Losing a Buck

Once you've grown from straddling every role in the company yourself, you'll likely have separate departments for things like Finance, HR, Sales and Marketing, Operations and Customer Service.

The Finance Director will have the accumulative company budget, but each department will have its own. There is little point in giving Sales & Marketing a budget in January and then checking back in December to find out they've gone miles over it.

RULE of **THUMB**

Budgets should be
monitored daily.

That doesn't mean you have to email the FD every time you expense a new laptop or post a Facebook ad. Once again, we're back to processes. Each department will be trusted with its own budget; however, when a variable occurs, it's time to report it.

For example, perhaps each department is instructed that if their budget varies by 3% on any given day or week (depending on the type of business), they will have to inform the FD of the reason why it's gone up or down. Maybe there were train strikes that weekend, so fewer people made it to your screening. Whatever the reason, you phone the FD.

"Just a heads up, Sam. We're 35% down this weekend because the trains aren't running. We've had quite a few people move their tickets as well, so it might affect the next couple of weekends, too."

"Okay, good to know. Let's check back in this time next week and see how it's going."

Now, you've not only explained the revenue drop but also given Sam a heads-up about the knock-on effect. She won't be sitting in her office looking at the numbers and wondering why her graphs are more up and down than Santa's satchel.

The following month, maybe you spot something else, only this time it's positive, so you drop Sam an email:

Hey Sam,

Good news!
We had a wealthy client come in this week, so you may spot a spike in revenue.
We had to restock from the warehouse twice!
Honestly, there was so much champagne flying around I thought I'd won the Grand Prix.
Anyway, thanks to them, we were 6% over our target for the week.

Best Wishes

Sam now knows why the revenue has increased. She can also expect more outgoings than usual as both the venue and the warehouse will need to replenish their stock. Since a lot of the purchases are on 30-day credit, Sam knows that while she can see additional income now, she might not see the outgoings for another few weeks.

The trick for this kind of budgeting is implementing processes: set each budget-holder a threshold, so when it's breached you can start to understand the nuances of your operation. Three per cent is an arbitrary figure, of course. You can choose a suitable threshold depending on how volatile your market is and by using trial and error to see what works and what doesn't. If nothing abnormal happens for a few weeks, a scheduled monthly budget check-in should be sufficient.

A good analogy for budgeting is to see the FD as the person with the whole book, while everyone else gets a page. At first, some staff may feel their page is less important than the others, but in the context of the whole story, it might be the piece that helps everything else make sense.

Cash Flow

If you cut off the blood supply to any part of your body, first it'll stop working, then it will wither and die. Similarly, without cash, every part of your business will suffer. Like pebbles in a pond, the effects will ripple further than the eye can see, and sooner or later, nothing is left untouched.

* * *

Jake's got a candle business. Thanks largely to his TikTok audience, he's made almost £1,000 a week on average, rounding off the year at roughly £50,000 in revenue. His overheads are relatively low right now; the marketing's free, and he operates almost entirely from his kitchen. There are no staff, although he does have a few friends and family helping him out with packaging and labelling. Luckily, for the moment at least, he's paying them with a mixture of undying gratitude and free candles. As such, Jake's made almost 20% profit from his first year of trading, and he's already got some more funds in the bank from next season's pre-orders.

Since this is still his side hustle, he's not paying himself yet, so he decides to reinvest every penny in stock. He's confident that he'll be able to push the revenue to £75,000 and reasons that having hundreds of candles ready to go in his cupboard is just what he needs to get ahead of the demand. Thanks to buying in bulk, he's also got cheaper prices, which means his profit margin could grow even further this year.

When Jake has a bath that night, he lights one of his *Serenity Bliss* candles and daydreams about being in big stores all over the country. He doesn't know it yet, but in a little under six months, his business will be insolvent.

Producing in bulk certainly has its downsides. There is very little space in London flats, especially when you're sharing with two other people. Not only is he monopolising the kitchen hobs, but there's nowhere to store anything, and his housemates are constantly tripping over boxes whilst struggling to open their own fridge.

Before he has time to worry about their protestations, though, there are more pressing issues at hand. *Serenity Bliss* and *Girl Wonder* continue to sell steadily, but *Declutter* hasn't shifted a single unit. Why, then, he ponders while shaving one morning, did he decide to make 500 of them? The irony isn't lost on him, either. He's four months into his year, and *Declutter* has done absolutely nothing but take up shelf space.

Unfortunately, this isn't the end of Jake's woes. He's been asked to participate in a series of lucrative markets on the south coast; the problem is he can't afford the pitch fee or even the travel to get there. He's already exhausted the Bank of Mum and Dad, so he gets a payday loan. The interest rate is higher than a stag do in Amsterdam, but it's too good an opportunity to pass up, and he firmly believes he can sell his way out of trouble.

The market goes well, and Jake manages to shift around 40% of his stock. At the end of a long weekend, he packs his car and decides he's earned a pint before the drive back to London. He doesn't want to pay for more parking, so he finds a little side road and leaves the car there. Back in the pub, he bumps into some other market vendors, and they get carried away chatting about their passion projects.

When he finally returns to the car a few hours later, something's wrong. The light's on. Why would the light be on? *Wait, are the doors open?* Then it hits him! His car's been ransacked. While Jake paces around, wondering what to do, he can't help but picture them. Somewhere on the streets of Bournemouth, there's a criminal outfit running around with a few hundred quid of his cash, his spare wheel, and eight boxes of candles.

"It's okay, Jake," his dad says at the end of the phone. "At least you're not hurt. Just contact the police, and we'll see about making a claim."

Jake sighs. "You're right, I guess." He looks through the window into the footwell by the back seat. "Oh, wait! They've left something."

"You what?" his dad replies.

Jake swings the car door open. "I left the money box in with some of the candles. Maybe, just maybe."

He presses the phone against his shoulder with

his head and lifts the box to the back seat. He braces himself for a moment and then whips off the lid.

"Jake!"

For a moment, he can't speak.

"Jake, what is it?"

As tears begin to swell in his eyes, all Jake can manage is, "Oh, no!"

"Jake! What's wrong?"

The phone drops from Jake's shoulder, and his dad's worried voice fades into the distance. Jake is left staring at the only thing he has left, a box full to the brim of *Declutter* candles.

As he drives home that evening, he remembers the loan; he thinks about the tax bill he still hasn't settled and the late invoices he was hoping to pay on Monday. *This could be it,* he thinks, *it's all over.*

Now, you could say Jake was unlucky, and I'm sure most people wouldn't argue with that. But when you look a little closer, you'll see that he made a series of bad decisions because he didn't have the cash. He invested too much in stock and didn't put enough weight in having money he could spend when he needed it.

It's no different from getting your monthly paycheck and spending every penny on a grocery shop. Okay, you've got 25 cans of chickpeas, but you only eat them when you're trying to impress your parents, and they come over three times a year. What are you going to do with the rest?

Maybe you've stocked up on toilet roll in case there's a zombie apocalypse. Who knows, it might happen; we've certainly been through some strange times in recent years. But what if it doesn't? You've got six industrial-sized containers of bog roll that, unless you have some alarming health issues, will take about a decade to get through.

What happens if your boiler breaks, you crack a tooth, or your daughter decides to get married in Tobago? How are you going to pay for it when all your money is tied up in supplies you don't even need yet.

RULE OF THUMB

Don't have lines
that never move.

When you're setting your budgets at the beginning of the year, you've got to think, *How much do we need in the bank?* Is it a year's turnover? Six months?

If you're staring at your budget sheet and wondering why your stock lines never seem to change, you've probably bought too much. You need to learn to manage your resources. Clients pay late; the economy slows down, the council digs up the road right in front of your recording studio; whatever the reason you're having a tough month, your staff will still need to be paid on time and in full (and, ideally, so will your bills). You can only push your supplier's payments back so far because they're in the same position as you; without the cash, they can't trade, and if they can't trade, how can they fix your broken toilet, your website or your staffing issues? For better and for worse, we're all connected.

Good Debt / Bad Debt

We're often taught in school that debt is a bad thing, but it's extremely hard to grow a business without it.

In fact, because entrepreneurs quickly realise how vital cash flow is, they get to the point where they think, *Why would I purchase anything outright*? Why buy a vehicle when I can lease it and hang onto my cash a bit longer?

As with all things in life, there's a balance. You can't pay for everything upfront, and sometimes taking on a lease just makes more sense. However, when you're looking to get the best deal, money talks, and *all the money right now* speaks loudest of all.

You always want to negotiate from a position of strength. You know cash flow is integral to your own business, so it must be important to others. Why not take that knowledge into your negotiations? If everyone else is paying on a 30-day invoice or angling for lines of credit, how powerful is it to be the one customer who can say, "How much will you charge if I pay 100% upfront?"

The question isn't *Should I or shouldn't I take on debt?* it's *When do I?*

This, my friends, is where we need professional advice. Most people don't go to an accountant and ask for help; they just give them all their paperwork at the end of the year and wait for the bill. Then the accountant says, "Why didn't you claim tax relief on this?"

And you just look at him and say, "The same reason I didn't use a gap wedge for the first five years – I didn't know it was a thing."

Continuing the golf analogy for a moment, a good accountant should be your caddie; they should be involved *before* you make the decision, not after you've sliced your Pro V1 into the water hazard. Think of them as part of the strategy.

The law often isn't as restrictive as you think. There are all sorts of funding opportunities and tax advantages, but only if you know where to look.

It's true that you're likely to pay more for a lease than if you purchased a product outright. But there's more to it than that. Have you factored in that a lease might reduce your corporation tax liability? So, although you'll pay more for the product, you'll actually pay less when you look at the bigger picture.

Let's say you need a few company cars for your employees. When do they become commercial vehicles? What's the definition? The accountant might say, "No, don't buy a car; buy a van. You won't convince the government it's a work vehicle if you get a car."

Accountants can tell you the pros and cons of renting an office, joining a co-working space or becoming your own landlord. Before you spend £300 on your client's dinner, check what the taxman wants to know. Can you expense the drinks? (The answer's no, by the way.) Do you need to keep a record of who, why and where? What about if someone takes you for dinner? Should *that* be on your tax return?

At first, you'll pay an accountant more than you want to, but if you've selected the right one, they'll cover their costs many times over. Ask them to give you a format to start tracking your figures. Perhaps you see them once a month at first, then once a week. Before you know it, you might be hiring a finance director.

The lesson here is to utilise all the tools you have at your disposal. Speak to your accountant, show your figures to the bank manager, and investigate lines of credit. Get yourself in a healthy position so that if the worst happens, you're not standing on a street corner, far from home, crying into your last box of candles.

The Disaster Fund

I knew Covid was coming.

I don't mean that in a Bill Gates kind of way. I didn't know it was called Covid. But I've been in business for almost 50 years, and I can confidently tell you something is always coming. In 2009, they called it Swine Flu. In 1987, we had Black Monday. In 1973 and 2005, there were bombings in London. In 2001, there was an attack on the World Trade Centre. The oil crisis in the '70s led to a recession. Then there was another recession in the '80s. The dot-com bubble burst in 2000 (not to mention the hysteria around Y2K and the Millennium bug). What about the subprime mortgage crisis in 2007?

And it's not just catastrophic events with global ramifications you have to worry about, either.

> # RULE OF THUMB
>
> You need a
> disaster fund.

The Olympics coming to your city could spell a triumph or a disaster, as your regular trade could be disrupted by a machine way outside of your control. Your industry might be phased out (or eradicated) by technology. Your business partner might have a fall and never make it back to work.

You don't know what it's called, and, of course, you can't predict the finer details. In 2020, we had no idea we'd be locked up in our houses for months at a time, overdosing on instant coffee and resigning ourselves to haircuts that made us look like the cast of *This Is England*. But we knew something was coming, especially when cities like Milan started announcing lockdowns. So, how prepared were we?

Think of your disaster fund as your reserve

parachute. With any luck, you won't need it, but if and when you do, it'll be the only thing stopping you from falling flat on your face.

The target amount for such a fund will vary based on your turnover, profit and market volatility, but as an example, it may represent a year's worth of profit. If you have 100K in the bank and nothing happens in 12 months, you roll it forward and add another 10%. For the next year, you then have £110,000 in your war chest. If you don't delve into it that year either (praise the Lord), you roll it over again.

You may be thinking: *Well, that's all very well for you to say, but I can barely afford to get through the Tube barrier at Oxford Circus every morning. How are we going to set aside a disaster fund?*

Well, I'm afraid, if that's the case, you're on borrowed time. Something *will* happen: a burst water main in the high street, a fire that redirects people away from your café, or scaffolding that spoils the views you've advertised. How many businesses have the train strikes finished off I wonder?

If you can't save 10% a year, just save something, *anything,* until you're making enough revenue to up the percentage. If it helps, think of the disaster fund as a shareholder in the business. There's you, your co-founder, the tax office, and the company. Why should the company be any less financially stable than the rest?

I spent most of my career earning less than all the directors in my business. I was happy living within my means, knowing that if and when I sold, I would see the big payday. I made the company as strong as I could, for as long as I could.

When something goes wrong and you can still cover the wages and bills (even if you're just scraping by for a while), you won't have to make decisions based on panic. You will avoid having to make personal guarantees on impossible loans that may help you survive in the short term but will contribute to a slower and much more painful demise.

In 1989, a pleasure boat called *Marchioness* sank on the River Thames after being struck by *Bowbelle*, a two-thousand-tonne dredger. My best friend, Stevie, lost his life; as captain, he went down with his ship. Fifty of his passengers died alongside him, and 79 people were rescued from the water.

Despite being at fault, *Bowbelle* didn't stop or deploy her life rafts. In fact, she didn't even slow down. As she sailed forth towards the gloomy horizon, she took a whole industry with her into a darkness that it never recovered from.

The incident shook the public's confidence. Who wants to take their colleagues, friends, and loved ones anywhere such a tragedy could occur? Daytime ticket sales were affected for many years, and the post-1am boat parties never returned.

Of course, the human cost was the real tragedy here, but the knock-on effect was far reaching. Dozens of businesses that weren't even involved that night were forced to close. Vessels could no longer sell enough tickets, caterers lost big contracts, staff were let go and dreams were shattered. No one was prepared for it.

Looking back now, it's clear that health and safety standards of 40 years ago weren't up to scratch, even for the time. No one predicted it, but perhaps we should have, the signs were there.

Despite all my warnings, I assure you, it's not just doom and gloom out here. It may sound like there are constant blocks in the road, but as Marcus Aurelius said, "What stands in the way becomes the way." Maybe you have to sacrifice the flash car and the expensive holidays, but if you can keep your company strong and make it through the train strikes, a terrible summer, or a recession, there's so much light at the other side. Your competitors have had the same struggles, only they weren't prepared for the rain. One day, you might look up and see that the sun is shining and all their customers are banging on *your* door, with nowhere to go but here.

Critical Financial Distress

In the early days of starting your business, you need to be tough on collecting the money you're owed. As we've already discovered, everybody's in the same position; they're all trying to hold on to their cash. Your customers' payment terms may be 30 days, but it's been six weeks already, and you still haven't heard a peep.

They say closed mouths don't get fed; they don't get paid either. You can't just rely on the goodwill of others to send you what you're owed, especially if the person you're liaising with isn't actually the one signing off the payments. Phone your clients. Explain that you're a new business and that prompt payment is crucial. Most companies will be sympathetic and bump you to the top of the pile, while everyone else, well, what's another week between friends?

Now, the less cynical amongst you may be thinking that suppliers who don't chase their invoices will be rewarded for their patience; perhaps they'll be paid on time and given extra work.

"Sally's so great, isn't she? She never complains about late payments. Let's send it early this month and give her a little bonus on top," said no one... ever.

More often than not, your clients have every intention of paying you, but priorities can change in a heartbeat. They might be hovering over the transfer button at the end of the month, only to be distracted by an email. The subject reads LEGAL ACTION FOR LATE PAYMENT. Who are they going to pay first? Who would you pay first?

Please don't take this as free rein to plague your clients' social media comments with jibes like, "Shouldn't you be sending me some cash?" or "I keep refreshing my emails, but I see no remittance!"

The answer isn't to threaten your clients every time they're a few days late, but you must stay in communication with them. Speak to your contact first and see if they can chase the right person. They'll likely have the good grace to be embarrassed, so you can leave it with them for a day or two. Next, you can contact the finance team directly. But don't just approach them meekly with your name and business; have your invoice number and a project reference ready, and, as always, be prepared to ask the right questions.

"I'm so sorry, Sally. I don't seem to have a record of that invoice. Could you resend it?"

Classic! There's a possibility this is true, of course, but there's about the same probability that it's a delaying tactic. The key is to be assertive.

"Sure! No problem, Ernie. Sending that over now. The invoice was actually due two weeks ago. Is there any chance you can run the payment today?"

"Oh, I'm not sure about that, but I can try my best.

Let me investigate what's happened, and I'll come back to you."

It's a good start, but you can't leave it there. At the very least, you need to get Ernie to commit to when he'll next contact you. That way, if you don't hear back, he can expect another call.

"Thanks, Ernie," Sally says. "Between me and you, I run a small business, so it would mean a lot to me if you could rush this one through. If, for whatever reason, you can't pay the full amount, could you send me 50% today and the balance later in the month?"

"I hear you, Sally. Again, sorry you've had to chase. Like I said, leave it with me; I'll make it a priority."

"Thank you," Sally says. "Oh, and when can I expect to hear from you?"

Ernie pauses for a moment. "Tomorrow morning," he replies. "Absolute latest!"

"Great. Thank you."

Sally receives an email a few hours later saying the full amount is on its way. Ernie signs off with, *Next time, send the invoice to me direct ;)*

There's no reason you shouldn't get a positive response. You've provided a service, and your customers will know they are required to pay. They're in the same position with their clients, after all.

If you don't get a helpful reply, that's a red flag! Perhaps they're struggling to pay their bills, or maybe it's an unscrupulous business strategy. Whatever the reason, it looks like you could be in for a few restless nights in bed, tossing and turning with worry. You know what will help now, though, don't you? A disaster fund.

At some point, you will have a client who can't or won't pay. If they go into liquidation, it's actually illegal for them to give you any money. As tempting as it might be to go knocking on their door, they're not lying when they say it's out of their hands. That debt is now settled by the administrators, who decide how much each creditor receives. Unfortunately, there's a list, and just like all those nightclubs you queued outside in your teenage years, the VIPs pull up in their limousine and march straight to the front while you're out there shivering your butt off, wondering if you're even going to get through the door.

Secured creditors get the first bite of the cherry; these are the banks and lenders with collateral for their loans. Then, of course, the staff need their wages, holiday pay and pension contributions. And who can forget HMRC and their VAT, PAYE, NI, and all the other acronyms that take all your M.O.N.E.Y?

After all of that, you might get a look in, but by that point, we're talking months (maybe years) down the road and only pennies on the pounds. Through no fault of your own, your business could now be in 'critical financial distress', and suddenly, you're the one not paying your suppliers on time – and so the circle of life continues.

So, how do we minimise our risk?

1) Put it in your budget

Once again, we're talking about our disaster fund. Allow a percentage of your turnover to be put towards bad debts and do your best to chase payments when they're due.

2) If you can't afford it, don't give it

Not every client is right for your business. They may be a well-known brand and willing to pay over the odds, but if they're asking for 90 days' credit, you have to work out if you can afford to prop up *their* business with *your* cash flow. Is anyone giving you 90 days to pay? If not, why are you giving it to other people? All you're doing is funding their business. You're not a bank (unless you are).

3) Diversify your client base

Imagine if your biggest client was Wilko or Blockbuster. You had the credos of putting their logos on your website, and they paid good money. But then they go bust, and suddenly you've lost 60% of your revenue. As best you can, you need to spread your risk. Richard Branson's Virgin isn't one brand; it's a group of hundreds of smaller business entities spread across multiple industries, so if one card falls, the whole house doesn't come tumbling down.

4) Craft your Terms and Conditions

Speak to your accountant and see what document they can produce to help protect you from bad debts. Should the client pay you in full before you offer them the product or service? If not, how much can you ask for upfront?

If you're selling venue space at Christmas, what happens if your client cancels the day before? There's no way someone's going to replace them with 24 hours' notice, and you've now lost one of your most lucrative days of the year. So, what are your cancellation terms? Should you charge 100% of the venue fee? What about the catering costs and the production you've hired in? What if they cancel *three* months before the event? Should they still pay 100%? You still have time to fill the space, so perhaps you could lower it to 75%.

However robust your contract is, you'll always have some clients who want to negotiate the terms, so make sure you know what everything means and what purpose they serve. If a clause is wildly in your favour and you can't explain what it is, at best, you will look incompetent; at worst, you'll lose all credibility.

Everyone should know what they're signing up for. So, pull out the important points beforehand and explain what they mean. The first time they hear about their liabilities shouldn't be when something's gone wrong. "They should have read the small print" isn't a good enough argument.

RULE OF THUMB

A contract is only worth what you can enforce.

If you can't afford lengthy legal battles, then, in a way, the fairer you can make it, the safer you are. If you deal with lots of clients and the same clauses keep coming up, then you might need to iterate. Get good advice from professionals, learn when to fight your corner and where to make concessions. Your Ts and Cs should become more transparent, stronger and fairer every year, protecting both your business *and* your clients.

Insolvency

In any test to become a director, insolvency (when your business is unable to pay its debts) would be essential to learn about. Red flags to look out for include: cash flow problems, declining revenues, lousy credit, increasing debt, or emails threatening legal action.

RULE OF THUMB

Don't be afraid to ask for help.

It's illegal to trade when you're insolvent, so if you find yourself in a position where there's not enough money to pay your staff or suppliers, speak to an accountant as soon as possible.

* * *

Bertie's Tours is a coach operator running routes across the UK. Starting out with one second-hand vehicle, Bertie has grown the business to a fleet of five coaches. Each coach lasts up to a decade, so every other year, he retires one and leases another. Thanks to this strategy, there's always a new coach on the lot, and the others are roughly two, four, six and eight years old.

The vehicles cost roughly £300,000 when new, so he has no desire to pay for them upfront. As such, his strategy is to lease-purchase. He pays a deposit, five years of monthly instalments and a balloon payment at the end. This means he's always making repayments on at least two of the coaches.

In the summer, business is booming, and several times in the last few years, Bertie has considered adding to his fleet. But as the winter rolls around and his revenue drops, he's once again thankful he hasn't overcommitted himself.

In the quieter months, Bertie faces many tough

decisions. His overheads are bleeding his cash dry, and he desperately searches for ways to reduce them.

Some days, he's only got two coaches going out, so perhaps he needs to get rid of a couple of drivers during the quieter times. If he were to do this, though, some of them might not be around by next season, which means hiring and training new staff all over again. He could retain their services (paying them not to work elsewhere), but that'll mean losing more money every day. How long can he keep that up? He still has his rent, vehicle payments, maintenance, storage and marketing to consider. He's been through this many times before, but it's still a stressful few months of balancing his books while waiting for business to pick up.

Thanks to his business savvy and dogged determination, Bertie makes it through the quiet season all the way to the doorstep of summer. Unfortunately, the weather doesn't get the memo. For the next 12 weeks, the sun behaves like a moody teenager, swooping in and out without much ceremony and never staying long enough to show any warmth. People give up on coach tours and city breaks and decide to go abroad.

After his worst summer on record, autumn fares no better, and the Stark words, "Winter is coming" begin to haunt him. Without enough bookings, the banks won't extend Bertie's loans, and the asset finance companies are panicking because he's missed a few payments. Soon, they want their collateral, but without coaches, Bertie has no business.

Perhaps he can sell one of his older vehicles second-hand? But will his business model work with less capacity? Either way, he won't be able to avoid redundancies now. While he chews it back and forth in his mind, a more immediate problem arises. He's got four trips to make today but no money for fuel. He also knows that unless he sells 100 more tickets this week, he won't be able to pay his drivers.

Then he gets an email: *Due to critical repair works, we've been forced to close the castle for the next two weeks.*

Two of his coaches are dedicated to that route, and now the main destination is lost. It's at this point Bertie knows he must down tools. For a long time, he's been a zombie business, staggering along, and just like the undead, all he's doing from here on out is damaging anyone he comes into contact with. After 15 years, Bertie's Tours is insolvent.

Bouncing Back

The truth is, you can do all the right things – manage your cash flow, control your budgets, fill up your disaster fund – and things can *still* go wrong. Every single company can make a profit or a loss very quickly due to outside influences that don't reflect whether you're actually good or bad at business.

You have to take ownership and accountability, but you should also realise that some things are out of your control. Interest rates rising when you're borrowing money, for instance, means you have to make more profit just to be where you were previously. Suddenly, you can't pay your suppliers, and you have a County Court Judgement against your name. Now, when new suppliers and lenders do a check, they won't give you credit. A government can do quantitative easing and just print more money. As a business, you can't do that. If oil prices go up, it affects the price of petrol and diesel, and once again, Bertie must either take the hit or put his prices up.

How many times have you received a pay rise at work only to find that your rent has increased by the same amount? If you're not already drowning in debt, it can feel like you're always treading water.

Markets are volatile; they move up and down, and it's so difficult to predict what will happen. What you need is information. Join a trade organisation and get active in your field. Not everyone needs to be a leading voice or a thought leader, but the more you surround yourself with people lobbying for your industry, the more you'll be able to plan for changes in legislation that will affect your ability to do business.

When Wilko Went South

In 1930, JK and Mary Wilkinson launched a hardware shop in Leicester that would one day turnover £1.43 billion per year. The growth of Wilkinson could be partly put down to their willingness to lean into the trends of the age. In the '40s, they used motorised transport to deliver their goods. In the '50s, their latest products targeted the nation's newfound love for DIY and home improvements. In the '70s, they transitioned from 'hardware stores' to a 'home and garden retail shop', with their own Wilko-branded products starting to emerge. In the '80s, they decided to do away with the bulkier items and focus instead on goods customers could take away with them in a bag. By the turn of the Millennium, they had 152 shops across the UK.

Fast forward to November 2023, and Lisa Wilkinson – former chair of Wilko and the granddaughter of the founder – gave oral evidence to the House of Commons Business and Trade Committee on the retailer's collapse. At that hearing, it was confirmed that more than 400 stores had been lost, approximately 12,000 jobs had been cut, and the company faced significant debt along with a pension-fund deficit of around £50 million. It was also revealed that the Wilkinson family had taken roughly £77 million from the business over the prior decade.

When asked why Wilko collapsed, Ms Wilkinson

said: "In essence, Wilko failed because we ran out of cash. That is what caused the downfall in the end." She highlighted multiple contributing factors – falling customer demand, high operating costs, rising rents, supply-chain challenges, the cost-of-living squeeze, and weakened lending and supplier support – but ultimately pointed to a cash shortage as the final blow.

There's that little thing called cash flow rearing its head again. It's as crucial to the candle maker as it is to the multi-billion-pound corporation. But I wonder, when did they stop thinking ahead? When did that desire to be at the forefront of the modern age disappear? And it's not just Wilko; what about Woolworths, Blockbuster and HMV? When did they stop innovating? Where was the succession planning? Who was the first person in the company's upper echelons underqualified for their position?

You don't get to this stage of collapse without a decade of knowing it's coming. What was your graph telling you? The first time your line stopped, levelled out and came down, what did you do? Did anyone say, "How do we get out of this mess? Why have we got stores in these locations? How do we fix it?"

The exorbitant rents, long leases and business rates were all cited as contributing factors by Lisa Wilkinson. Were they resistant to change? While their competitors focused on retail complexes with car parks, Wilko seemed to dig in on the high street. Why didn't they move quicker?

If you don't learn from your competitors, who else are you looking at? If the leases were becoming a problem, why not follow McDonald's and start purchasing the freeholds? McDonald's wasn't obsessing over the hamburger money – that belonged to the franchisees – they were in the property game.

If Wilko was trapped in long leases in the wrong locations, what could they do? Well, something is better than nothing. Perhaps they could sell the least profitable shops. The market won't panic when you sell a handful of your 400 stores. But even if you have to shut 200 shops, surely that's better than letting a third-generation business fall into a black hole.

RULE OF THUMB

If you can see it happening, don't wait.

I visited a Next recently; it was heaving. They had a coffee shop inside where people could sit with their families and take a break from shopping. Why couldn't Wilko do a joint venture with Starbucks or Costa and have a coffee shop in every store? Maybe they could have added a soft play centre or food and beverage outlets that would attract people to the location. Maybe they could apply to the council for a change of use and convert one of the spaces into a VIP cinema. The lesson here is to do *something*. Your management figures will tell you if you have a problem. How often are you reviewing them?

You've got to ask the right questions. What are our competitors doing? How can they be cheaper *and* offer better quality products than we do? Where are they located? Where are they seeing success? Why are we taking dividends when we need money to invest in making our shops fit for purpose?

If one shop has just five thousand square feet and makes £2 million per year, and another has two million square feet but generates the same revenue, which business is better? The first is making £400 per square foot; the second is making just £1. How many square feet did Wilko have?

Take Richer Sounds, for example. The legendary home entertainment retailer made the *Guinness World Records* when its first store in London Bridge was accredited with the highest sales per square foot of any retailer in the world. At its peak, it made £20,870 per square foot (or £195,426/m²).

Wilko knew they needed smaller locations, but were they doing anything about it? Were they selling sites, closing stores, or subletting to key cutters, dry cleaners or a local yoga club? There was nothing that looked like they were aiming to maximise the square footage.

"We were about to enter into secured lending arrangements with Macquarie when the 2022 mini-Budget happened," Ms Wilkinson said. "We were literally in the midst of that. At that point, the interest terms on that loan were hiked massively, and that became infeasible."

One way or another, internal factors are a major reason why businesses fail. It's not Lisa Wilkinson's fault; the mistakes could have been made two generations before her. Where was the training? Where was the succession planning? No matter how big you are, external factors like a change in interest rates could easily stunt your growth, but if your company is poorly run, it could completely wipe you out.

Chapter 4

Buying and Selling

What Can We Learn from Lonnie's Lawn Mowers?

Lonnie's Lawn Mowers was an institution. If you needed gardening equipment in the late '90s and you were within a 25-kilometre radius of his shop, Lonnie's was where you went. Everybody liked him; he was smart, funny and kind. If you ever had a problem with one of his products, even many years after you bought it, he'd always go above and beyond to help.

A lot of people are nice, though, but they can't all do what Lonnie did; it takes something else. As he became more experienced, Lonnie knew that his personality alone wasn't enough to grow a strong business – he had to adapt.

The model was simple at first. Customers would come in, look around, and if Lonnie got to talking, chances are they'd buy a lawn mower. There wasn't much else he offered at the time, though, other than some spare parts and a stack of garden gnomes by the kiosk.

The problem that haunted him at night was the sheer number of new people he needed to get through the door. However well he got on with everyone who came in, unless they were moonlighting as a groundskeeper, he might not see them again for 10 years. I mean, really, how often do you buy a lawn mower? Especially when the last one cost £400 and was from a reliable chap like Lonnie. They last forever!

It was time to diversify. The landlady had been trying to sell the empty shop next door for months. For whatever reason, the deals kept falling through, and she was pulling her hair out at the thought of how much money it was costing her – and not just from the lack of rent.

An empty property can be a security nightmare. If someone breaks into your building, urinates on your floor, slips on it, and cracks their head on the concrete, *you* could get sued for it. Even if you win the case, it could cost you thousands in legal fees.

What if they break in, make themselves a tea, and decide they like it so much they're going to stay? Then what? If squatters occupy your premises, you could have a hell of a job trying to get them removed. It's not like you can just go in there, grab them by the collar, and throw them out, either. I mean, you can try, but you're the one who could end up in prison.

Imagine being a landlord and bringing a potential operator down, only to be locked out of your own venue. You're peering through the window saying, "You see that sleeping bag?"

"Which one?"

"The one by the decks with all the ashtrays on top."

"Ah, yeah, I see it."

"The toilets are just behind there."

"Riiight! Okay. When do you think it'll be available for me to, you know, actually go in."

"Absolutely no idea! It's great, though, isn't it? Shall we talk numbers?"

"Maybe just send me an email."

If you're willing to invest in suitable systems and the right people, security issues can be easily overcome. Of course, you have to pay the cost, and this will just be one of many.

First-time operators often forget about rates. Alongside your rent, your local authority will impose a tax based on your usage and square footage. Think of this as a much more expensive council tax, and without a tenant, landlords could be haemorrhaging money.

Up steps Lonnie. He's been reading, making calls,

and speaking to other business owners in the area, and all the while storing up knowledge. He knows to negotiate from a position of strength, and with all this information, he's in a very strong position indeed. He's just as desperate to expand as his landlady is to fill the space, but only one of them knows that.

Lonnie asks his accountant to call the agent who is looking after the property and anonymously enquire about the unit. When the information pack is sent through, he is flabbergasted. It's twice the size of his shop but almost triple the price. The accountant signs off his summary email with: *No wonder she can't find anyone to rent it.*

Lonnie decides the time is now. He drops the landlady an email about a leak he's been meaning to get fixed. A few days later, they share a cup of coffee as Lonnie shows her the most recent changes to the store and introduces her to his favourite gnomes (most of which he's named). As they sit down to finish their drinks, he deftly changes the subject.

"So," he sighs into his chest, "you know how much I love it here."

As he leaves the implication hanging in the air, her eyes widen like she's just swerved past oncoming traffic.

"There's still 18 months left on the lease," Sienna says, almost tripping over her words.

"No, of course, and I intend to honour it. It's just

I've been thinking about expanding, and there's simply not enough space here. We've found a place up the road that's perfect. So, if our offer gets accepted – fingers crossed – we'll wind down our operation here. I just wanted to let you know now so you have plenty of time to find someone else."

Lonnie begins to fill her in on his vision for the new location. He talks about the investment he's got coming in and his plans to increase footfall. Sienna shifts around anxiously in her chair. Eventually, she can't take it anymore.

"Lonnie, I'm sorry, let me stop you there. I had no idea you were expanding. If only either of us communicated a little better." It was her turn to sigh. "Let me... let me show you something," she says.

As they look around the site next door, Lonnie has to pinch himself several times. *This place is perfect,* he thinks. Outdoor space, a wall you could easily knock through to join the two shops, and a car park that stretches around the back of the building.

"This is so great, Sienna. I wish I'd seen it sooner. It's just... let me talk to my investor. It'll be a shame to move if we don't have to. How much are you charging?"

Sienna smiles, her shoulders dropping like she's finally starting to relax. "Lonnie, for you," she says, "I know we'll work something out."

Even at the massively reduced rate Lonnie

negotiates, he is solving so many problems for her. The background checks are already done; he has a history of paying on time and a great reputation. No more marketing costs, talking to agents every day, overnight security, or wasted time. Lonnie is even paying the rates. Sienna can finally focus on her other business interests.

Lonnie signs a new lease for both properties. He agrees to a fixed rent at a vastly reduced cost for two years and a step-rental for the following three, where the price will increase annually, ending up just shy of the current advertised rate. His brother-in-law invests £75,000 to help with the rent deposit and the fit-out, and they get to work.

While the build is happening, he's out taking care of inventory: seeds and fertilisers for the lawn, plants and soil for the flower beds, weed killer and jet washers for the patios and driveways, gardening tools, and even safety gear like goggles, gloves and ear defenders.

By the time Lonnie's Lawnmowers reopens, it's more like Lonnie's Landscapers. Later in this book, we'll discuss 'The four ways to grow your business', but, for the moment at least, Lonnie has his eyes set on two of them: *How can I get my customers to spend more money? What value can I add so they keep coming back?*

He became a master of packages. In the early

days, if you bought a lawn mower from Lonnie you were pitched a garden gnome, offered a warm handshake and given help carrying both to your car. Now, you needed a trolley. Customers could wander around an emporium of garden wonders, knowing everything they bought had a deal attached to it.

Buying a lawn mower for £200? Why not take our Lonnie's Lawn Care Package: a lawn mower, fertiliser and grass seed for £220? Got yourself some pruning shears? What about the Weekend Warrior Package that gets you the shears, garden gloves and heavy-duty bin bags for an extra tenner? How about Keeping Up Appearances? A hedge trimmer, a pressure washer and weed killer so your front garden becomes 'The envy of any nosey neighbourhood'.

As Ahmed studies the prices, he bites down on his lower lip like he's sucking poison from a snakebite. After a while, he looks up. "Why's everything always about packages with you, Lonnie?" he asks.

Lonnie's face is hidden by the hydrangea display, but from behind it, a smile percolates across his lips. "When was the last time you went to McDonald's and bought a bag of chips?" he asks.

"Every time!"

Lonnie's head appears from behind the flowers. "When was the last time you went to McDonald's and bought JUST a bag of chips."

Ahmed ponders for a moment. "Never!" he shrugs.

"How about just a burger?"

"Well, I dunno, maybe once or twice!"

"Exactly!" Lonnie says. If you're spending five pounds on a burger, what's another quid for chips and a drink?" With a quick snip of his shears, Lonnie trims his display and catches the wilting stems. "You save money" – snip, snip – "I sell more products" – snip – "everybody wins!" He stops to take a proud look at his handiwork. "It's beautiful, isn't it?"

Ahmed nods. "Yeah, it's a fair point. I hadn't thought of it like that. Give me the Peaceful Planter Package, then, please. And I'll have some of those garden bin bags while I'm here, too."

Lonnie smiles. "Great choice, Ahmed."

He rings up the items, and as the final price is displayed on the till, Lonnie's lips tip down in disappointment.

"What's wrong?" Ahmed asks.

"Oh, nothing," Lonnie says. "We do free delivery to the local area Monday to Wednesday now."

"Oh, brilliant. That would really help, actually. I was worried about all that soil; I might have had to make two trips."

Lonnie clenches his teeth and points to the sign behind him. FREE DELIVERY FOR ORDERS OF OVER £175.

"You've only spent £160," Lonnie says with a mischievous smile.

Ahmed's eyelids narrow for a moment. "Hmmm." He looks around. "I just don't think I need anything else."

"It's only five pounds for delivery, otherwise. Won't break the bank, will it?" Lonnie says, grabbing the bin bags.

"Yeah, but, you know, shame to miss out. Oh well, it's only..."

"Wait a second!" Lonnie says. "I've got just the thing," He bends beneath the counter and pulls up a box. "You're lucky, 'cos this is the last one."

Ahmed pokes his nose closer to get a better look. "What is it?" he asks.

"I call him Gordy," Lonnie says.

Ahmed laughs as he pulls out his wallet. "Let me guess, Gordy the garden gnome?"

"How did you know?" Lonnie says. "It must be fate." He flashes his infamous smile as he opens the box, takes Gordy out, and swivels him around proudly like an actor showing off his first Oscar to a friend.

"We'll find a good home for him, don't worry," says Ahmed.

Lonnie waves goodbye to Ahmed and finishes trimming the display. Just as he pops the shears back in their place, he notices a man walking around between the aisles; he has a small box of seeds in his hand and is eyeing up some garden gloves. Lonnie's new assistant, Alex, steps out from the back and starts walking towards him, but Lonnie catches her arm just in time.

"Not yet," he says. "Wait until he's looking for the third item."

"How do you know he'll—"

"Just watch."

The man flicks between sets of gloves for a moment or two before selecting a pair he likes. As he clenches them against the box of seeds, he drops one on the floor. He scoops to pick it up, turns the box sideways and balances the gloves on top, heading over to look at some plants.

"Okay," Lonnie says, "now's your time to shine!"

Alex smiles as she walks towards the entrance, not breaking a stride as she scoops up a basket and takes it over to the customer. She leans in to catch his eye as he negotiates a plant from the shelf.

"Ah, thanks so much," the customer says. "I only came in for seeds, but you know how it is."

"No problem," Alex replies. "I'm just over here if you need me for anything else."

That's all it takes. As Alex walks away, Lonnie knows the seed is already sown. He's been around retail enough to know that if he sees a guy in his mid-30s or above, more often than not, he won't get a basket. He'll come in for one item and end up stacking more and more in his arms until he's wobbling around like a circus performer with a chair balanced on his chin. There's nothing wrong with that per se, but Lonnie knows they only buy what they can carry. Give him a basket, and not only will he be grateful for the thought, but he'll likely fill it to the brim. This one trick alone has been responsible for dozens of extra items being purchased per week, and all he's doing is making people more comfortable as they shop. Eventually, he puts a row of baskets at the back of the shop for anyone who changes their mind halfway around.

Lonnie's customer service has always been second to none, but as he's expanded, his marketing has started to catch up. If you purchase anything, no matter how big or small, he finds a way to advertise on it. Whether it's his shop name sprayed on the side of your strimmer, his logo stuck next to the bar code on every bag of soil or the company details on your receipt, Lonnie wants you to remember where you bought your products so when you're sitting in the pub with a mate and they need a hanging basket for Mother's Day, there's only one name on everyone's lips.

When the shop's quiet, Lonnie doesn't rest idle; he's always thinking of ways to drum up more business. He likes to phone customers, see how their products are doing and invite them in for a coffee to check out the seasonal flowers. As much as he loves it, though, phone calls are very time-consuming. He knows he needs to find a more efficient way to contact people with his offers and upgrades.

He's recently hired a new employee to help expand his foliage, and this kid knows everything there is to know about plant care. *Wouldn't it be great,* he thinks, *if we could share monthly tips about types of soil, how often you water specific flowers, and how to cut plants to grow in a certain direction?*

Lonnie puts a sign at the front desk asking people to sign up for their newsletter, but he goes a step further. Previously, he'd give people a form to fill in when they got home so they could register for a guarantee. How many people actually bother, though? Chances are it ends up in a draw or lost in the black hole of instruction manuals and takeaway menus. To counter this, Lonnie creates a comfy spot in the shop where people can fill in any forms they need. He's made it part of the experience. You buy your product, sort out your guarantee, and in the meantime, everything's loaded into your car for you.

He's helped them out, sure, but in return, he now has their email address, birthday and home address. For repeat customers, he'll send birthday cards with discount vouchers and samples of new products he thinks they'll like. He sends weekly mailers out giving gardening tips and encouraging customers to shop for the season. He, of course, doesn't bother anyone who isn't interested, but why wouldn't keen amateur gardeners want to get more from the products they're buying?

Lonnie's smart: he knows that it's the customers who dictate how successful he is, so his mission has always been to make them feel special. For almost five years, one of his most loyal customers, Brian, would visit his shop once a week. But more recently, he only seems to come in once a month. The next time Brian pops in, Lonnie decides to check in with him.

"How are things, Brian? We miss you around here. I used to set my watch around your visits."

"Ah, I do miss it, Lon, but I'm almost 70 now. You won't see me out there digging up the weeds for much longer. I'm only pushing on because we can't deal with sitting out there when it's overgrown, and you know how much my Jenny loves a short lawn."

An imaginary light bulb appears above Lonnie's head. Since the expansion, he has plenty of professional gardeners and landscapers using the store. Why doesn't he create a preferred suppliers list for customers unable (or unwilling) to do certain jobs themselves? The gardeners could agree to come to him for their supplies, and he'll just kick over the referrals. He could take it even further. If you're not sure how to build a planter, one of our preferred gardeners can come in and set it up for you. Maybe he'll get enough work from it to employ someone full-time.

"You know what, Brian?" Lonnie says, "Leave it with me. I may have some ideas."

Brian chuckles behind his grey bushy beard. "You know what, Lonnie? I'd never doubt it for a second."

How to price your products?

How much do I charge? When you first start your company, this might be a troubling question. Where do you even begin?

Later in this book, you'll learn *The Four Ways to Grow Your Business*, which lays the foundations for any brand to generate more revenue. Further on, you'll read about *The Dentist Theory*, where we reverse engineer our prices from our desired income and pace of life.

Before we get to that, though, it's important to understand the basics. Here are five things you absolutely must consider before putting a number on your products or services.

1) Assess your overheads

You can't set your price until you know what it costs to open your doors and stay in business.

What are your running costs? Rent, staff, materials, insurance, software subscriptions, marketing – it all adds up. Then you have the undercover costs, the ones people often forget about: taxes, accountancy fees, and, of course, your disaster fund.

Ask yourself: *How much do I need to make to break even?* Then, *How much do I need to grow the business, invest in new opportunities, and pay myself?* Only when you have these numbers ready can you move on to the next step.

2) Assess the market

In order for your business to survive, you need to sell your products for more than they cost to make. That much is obvious, but how much is a fair and realistic amount to add on? In many cases, the industry you're operating in will guide you.

Supermarkets might make 5% gross profit on each sale, but they are shifting a high volume of products and have built a business model around customer necessity and routine behaviour. Software companies, on the other hand, might have margins of over 70%.

Once their product is built, it costs very little to sell one more; there's no warehouse, shipping or raw materials to worry about. Their business is built around scalability, where each additional sale generates huge profit.

Take a look at the typical margins in your field. How have they changed over the last 10 years? Are they stable? Are they heading in the right direction? If not, maybe you're in the wrong industry. If you started a business in 2010, hopefully it wasn't selling fax machines or DVDs.

Once you've assessed the industry as a whole, zoom in. What are your competitors offering? It's not just about what they're charging. How long have they been around? What's their standing in the marketplace? What additional benefits are their customers getting?

Now measure this information against your proposition. How do you match up? Can you offer better quality, a more personalised service, or tell a more compelling story? If you can, perhaps you're in a position to charge more. If you can't, maybe you need to be *the cheaper option*, so you can chip away at the market share by undercutting your opposition.

If you go down this route, you'll need to think about three things:

1. Can you afford it?
2. What does it say about your brand if you are "cheaper" or "the cheapest?"
3. How many more items would you need to sell?

It's easy to assume that the LOWER the price, the HIGHER the volume. So, if you sell something for less money, it'll be easier to get more people to buy it. But the question isn't "Can I sell more?" it's "How many more would I have to sell?"

3) Beware of the discount

It's tempting to slash prices to boost sales, especially when things go quiet. But just remember, every discount comes straight from your profit margin.

Let's say your product is normally sold at £100 and makes you 35% gross profit (£35). If you give a discount of just 10% (£10), it knocks off nearly a third of your profit.

So, what does this mean?

Well, in order to make up the difference, you'd have to sell a lot more units. But you can't just operate blindly. Have you any idea how much that discount will cost you? And therefore, how much more work you'll need to do to make it back?

Once again, the question isn't, "Can I sell more?" it's "How many more would I have to sell to get back the same profit?"

As you can see from the example below, if you sell 1,000 units at full price (£100) and make £35,000 profit, discounting by just 10% will cost you £10,000.

Scenario	Cost to You	Price to Customer (per unit)	Gross Profit (per unit)	Units Sold	Total Gross Profit
Full Price	£65	£100	£35	1000	£35,000
10% Discount	£65	£90	£25	1000	£25,000

Now, let's look at the bigger picture. How many more units do we need to sell to make that money back? If you knock 10% off your price, you no longer need to sell 1,000 units; you need to sell 1,400. Sit with that for a moment. Do you really think a 10% discount will persuade another 400 people to buy? That's 40% more.

It might. And it could be a big win for you. You may have signed up new customers, convinced them to subscribe to your email list, or had people send out referral links. You could put it down as a marketing expense or the cost of customer acquisition.

But what if it doesn't convince people? What if 10% just isn't persuasive enough? So, you get back in the boardroom and someone says, "Let's go with 30%. If I was buying, that would definitely convince me."

The question someone in that room has to answer is: How many more units would we need to sell to get back to the same position?

And the answer?

...600%.

If your profit margin is 35% and you give a 30% discount, you'll have to sell 7,000 units instead of 1,000.

At this point, it can feel like you've got heavy legs on a speeding treadmill. It's so hard to keep up, and any minute now you could lose your step and come crashing off into the free weights area. Before you discount *anything*, revisit our Rules of Thumb: "Don't Guess" and "Never Make it up."

If you're still finding this hard to visualise, take a look at the graph on the next page. On the left, you'll see how much more volume you'll need to sell by reducing the price, and on the right, how much less you'll need to sell if you increase it.

Price Changes vs. Volume Needed (Assumes 35% Profit Margin)

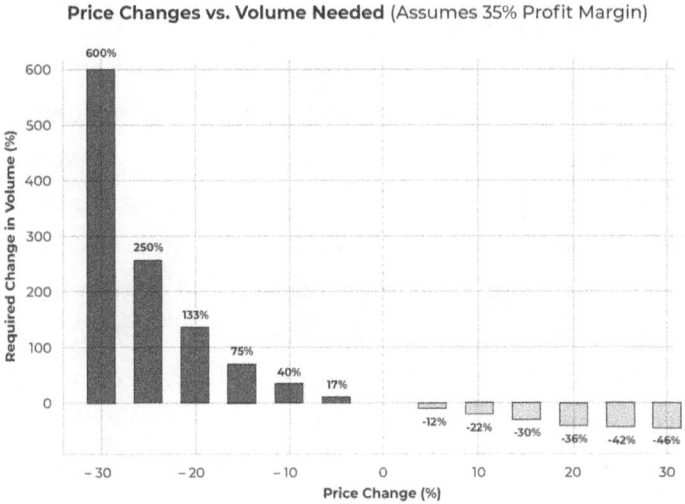

I'm not saying you can't discount. If it wins you a new customer or helps you get rid of old stock, perhaps you've done the right thing. But if you're going to do it, all I ask is that you think about the strategy. Instead of giving money off, can you upsell packages, offer perks, or partner with sponsors? If you still want to go down the discount route, that's fine, but how can you make sure it's happening at the right time?

Remember, there's no point in selling out if you're selling yourself short. So, run the numbers, understand the consequences and make an informed decision.

4) Seasonal pricing

You need to learn how to get the business when YOU need it. There's no use cramming more customers into your beer garden in the summer, when you've got nowhere to put them. At a certain point, the bars will be too full, your servers won't be able to walk anywhere without being crashed into and spilling drinks, and you'll actually make less money. And that's before we mention health and safety, customer experience, and staff satisfaction.

You need those crowds coming back on a cloudy day. How can you entice them in? What changes can you make to the venue? What packages and deals can you offer? If you've got corporate parties wanting a better price, tell them if they sign up for an event in January *now*, you'll help them out with the cost of their summer event too.

Seasonal pricing doesn't have to mean discounts; we've already seen the damaging effect they can have. It's far better to put your prices up in the summer than to put them down in the winter. If you go to a hotel in a city where the Olympics are on, you'll pay triple the price, not just for the bedroom but for the surrounding shops, restaurants and entertainment. Go to the same location in the off-season, and you'll be inundated with great deals and upgrades.

Customers are conditioned to pay more during

peak times, but it's always worth remembering that giving someone a huge discount doesn't alter their expectations. They'll still expect the same level of experience. Are you confident you can still deliver it at that price? Charging more will protect your margin, but it might just protect your service too.

5) A/B testing

Businesses use this method to compare two versions of something and determine which one performs better. In retail, for example, it could mean different prices, promotions, shop layouts, or packaging styles in two separate locations. Perhaps they're testing the wording for a snack promotion near the self-checkout machines. Store A gets "Buy One Get One Free" whilst Store B gets "15% off".

The goal is to observe real-world customer behaviour and measure the results. When supermarkets raise prices, they'll often A/B test in a busy high-street store to see how shoppers react. Chains in places like Barkingside, East London, have high foot traffic and a varied customer base, which makes them an ideal location for trials before rolling out any changes more widely.

On social media platforms like TikTok, Instagram, or LinkedIn, you might run the same ad but test it against two different audiences, helping you to narrow down your target market.

Audience A: Women aged 25–40 interested in wellness and parenting.

Audience B: Women aged 30–50 interested in finance and entrepreneurship.

You can then measure which group has a higher number of clicks, better engagement, or actually ends up purchasing your product. This will help you to refine your target market and spend your ad budget more efficiently.

Don't get decision paralysis. Set your prices, see how the markets respond, and react accordingly. Believe it or not, it is possible to overdo the market research. Sooner or later, you're just going to have to pull the trigger.

A Market of One

Many years ago, there was a premium cigarette company, let's call it Velvet Rose. The owner, Karim, wanted to try his hand in the tobacco industry. When it began, it wasn't a serious venture for him; it was more of a marketing exercise, so perhaps he was a bit more liberated than most business owners.

Cigarettes were cheap back then, maybe £2 per pack. But Karim wanted to challenge himself. Could he convince people to spend 10 times that amount? He sourced some sleek-coloured papers, crafted them into long and elegant shapes, and created a majestic-looking box to keep them in. Women in particular were drawn to the presentation and the status it gave them to be seen puffing one.

A wealthy client took such a liking to the product that they asked for their own range of Velvet Rose. But Karim was already overworked. His idea had risen further than he could have imagined, and he no longer had any room on his production line.

"I'll tell you what," Karim said. "If you pay me all the money upfront, I'll do it. It's the only way I can expand to meet the demand."

To Karim's surprise, the client agreed, and they took "The world's most expensive cigarettes" to the Middle East. Pretty soon, the biggest names in the industry wanted a piece of the action. They released their own premium ranges and charged £19 per pack, undercutting Velvet Rose by a pound.

How do you think they did? Did Karim have anything to worry about?

Well, my question is, who wants to buy the world's *second* most expensive cigarette? What kind of status symbol is that? Velvet Rose didn't have better tobacco or a smoother taste; it just had a stronger presentation.

If Karim had obsessed over market research, he never would have gotten to £20. He managed to reach the holy grail of business, where he wasn't competing on price or even quality with anyone; all he needed was *perception*. He created a category of his own and a market that came to him.

You don't always have to be the cheapest, or even the best, but wherever you stand, you must stand out.

Incremental Business

What is a Sales Target?

Managers might see it as a way to measure performance or an incentive to drive growth, while the sales team may think of it as an excuse to swagger around the office, pop champagne bottles, and tell everyone who'll listen how important they are to the firm.

What some of these people haven't worked out yet is that a target is a *minimum requirement* for you to cover your overheads to the business. You *should* be hitting your sales targets. It's not something that needs a ribbon-cutting ceremony every time you land on 100%. The time to celebrate is when you *crush* your targets, because everything over that minimum is when you and the company really see the reward for all your hard work.

The question you should ask yourself, at any level, is, 'Why would I sell something without enough margin to run the business?' Every deal needs a contribution to overheads.

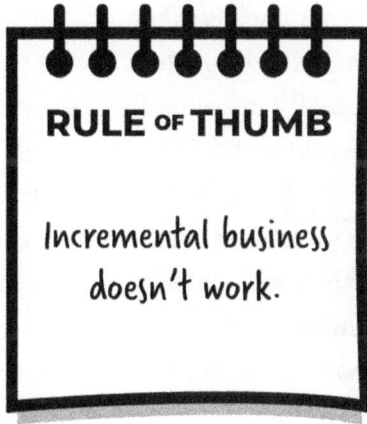

RULE OF THUMB

Incremental business doesn't work.

Incremental business is saying we'll make nothing from this deal, but we hope it translates to more work from this customer in the future. Of course, there are exceptions, but for every example you can find where it has paid off, there's probably another 50 where it's failed.

When people used to put a signed events contract on my desk at City Cruises, if the figures didn't stack up, I'd hand it right back.

"Where's your contribution to overheads?" I'd say.

"Oh, they do hundreds of events every year. If we can just show them what we're about, I'm sure they'll book another dozen with us next year."

"Oh, sorry, Tommy," I'd say, reaching out to grab the contract back. "Forgive me, busy day. I must have skim read it. What page is that on?"

Tommy's nervous laugh tells me he was expecting some pushback. "It's not actually *in* the contract. They told me on the phone they would, though."

I sigh. "Well, you can tell them on the phone that if they sign up to three events for next year, we'll drop the price for this one. Otherwise, we're not here to fund their summer party."

Tommy looks shocked, but the longer he spends in this business, the more he'll start to understand that if it's not written down, it doesn't exist. The time for a tour boat operator to give away a cheaper product is in the winter, not during their peak season. You want a better price for the summer? No problem! Book your January event with us at the same time, and we'll do a deal.

If our dinner party this Saturday is £35 per head, but we've only filled up two-thirds of the room, *that's* the time to run an offer. We've already covered our costs; from here on out, every bum on a seat is profit. Not to mention the atmosphere you'll get from a full room; it'll give the performers a boost, energise the rest of the crowd, and hopefully increase the bar revenue. Let's post an offer on social media: £25 per head for anyone booking by the end of the day!

Once again, it's not that you can't *ever* reduce your margins; it's that you can't *ever* guess.

Evaluating Stock

If your supplier raises prices, your profit margin will decrease. You then have a choice to make: Do you follow their lead and increase your rates, or swallow the loss so your customers won't pay more?

When he first opened, Lonnie bought lawnmowers for £110 and sold them for £155. If he were selling chocolate bars or hair wax, he'd likely have settled for a smaller percentage markup, but with big-ticket items, he had to factor in higher operational costs, including storage, transportation and maintenance.

He knew the importance of cash flow, so instead of having all his money tied up in stock, he only purchased a handful of models. He'd then show the customer a brochure and explain the differences of any that weren't on display. As a buyer, there's nothing quite like getting your hands on the actual product you're considering, but in the early days,

Lonnie had to prioritise managing his inventory and maintaining his cash. When he sold one of the in-store products, only then would he replace it.

Eventually, people began to hear about the mowers and his exceptional customer service, but Lonnie was still reluctant to put more money into his stock. He contacted the manufacturer one day to discuss pricing, only to hear that they'd all gone up.

The new cost for his best-selling model was £135, which meant that to return to his current profit levels, he needed to sell them at £180 instead of £155.

The next day, Lonnie got instant feedback.

"Can I help you?" Lonnie asks.

"Hey, yeah. My friend told me to come in and talk to you about a mower, but he told me it was £135. That looks like it over there, but it's much more expensive."

"No, that's the right one. The prices have changed, but it's still a bargain for what you're getting. That'll last you 10 years, that thing. What's that? 5p a day?"

The man laughs and says he'll think about it, leaving Lonnie to ponder.

How many shop owners would have just split the difference and sold it for £165 instead? Or let it go at the original price just to get rid of it? What Lonnie learned here was the importance of understanding the replacement value of his products. He shouldn't just ask himself what he paid for it; he needs to consider how much it would cost to replace it.

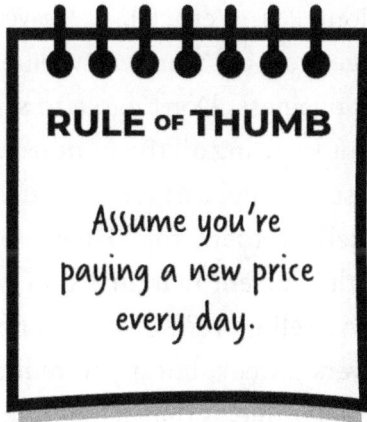

RULE OF THUMB

Assume you're paying a new price every day.

Get into the habit of evaluating your stock daily. Get to know your suppliers, what they're charging, how often their prices change, and by what percentage. Lonnie has options. He can work with a different manufacturer, reduce his inventory slightly, or even reshape his business model to focus on more profitable products.

In this instance, Lonnie wants to either increase his prices gradually or honour the old price to a handful of customers. He knows everything is worth a conversation, so he approaches his supplier.

"How many would I need to buy for you to sell at

the original price? How would that change if I paid upfront?"

The manufacturer is in the same position as you; they want your business despite the increase, so communication is crucial. However those negotiations go, you can't underestimate the cost of running your business. Don't agree to sell a product for less without knowing all the numbers. How much will they cost to replace? How much are your competitors selling them for? How much are you making with the current margins? Can you afford to make less if you sell more? Maybe you needed to sell two lawnmowers a week, but if you reduce the price, you'll need to sell three. Is that achievable?

Lonnie knew he couldn't be so reliant on one product, and so, as we saw earlier, he decided to expand. When he reopened, he had dozens of items from a plethora of different suppliers, which meant that constantly reevaluating his stock became more crucial than ever.

Best in Class

Have you ever stopped to think, *What does the pinnacle of my industry actually look like?* or *What does 'Best in Class' mean across different disciplines?'*

Having left school at 15 without any grades, I've always been a proponent of surrounding myself with people I can learn from. I was once part of a business lunch club, where members would congregate semi-regularly to talk about our recent wins or the hurdles we were facing. Sometimes, we'd read the same books and discuss them as a group, or we might watch sales and marketing videos together or invite an HR specialist, finance director or bank manager in to give a talk.

One afternoon, we took a field trip to Newcastle. We had no idea where we were going, only that the organiser was taking us somewhere that exemplified this month's theme: Best in Class.

We arrived by taxi, entering through an enormous gate and pulling up at a contemporary office block. I remember trying to figure out what the business might be – the building looked like it could house a private doctor's surgery or, if it were today, a David Lloyd gym. It was flanked on all sides by lush green gardens and colourful flowers, while the sound of dogs rolling over each other competed with the noise of the pebble driveway crunching beneath our feet.

I spotted the words 'Washington Kennels' embossed on a smart wooden sign by the door. As we arrived at reception, my head was on a swivel; it was nicer than most retirement homes. Everything was so clean and homely. To my right, there was a pet shop with all kinds of food and accessories. To my left was a charming hydro pool that looked so inviting I'd have quite happily belly-flopped into it. Behind the reception desk were a few courts with various canine games going on. I was just getting onto my tiptoes to try and steal a glance at the activities when the receptionist greeted us. For the next few hours, we got a tour of the facility and some insight into the history.

The owners, Spillers, had owned flour milling operations and bakeries since the early 19th century. In 1927, they introduced the Winalot dog biscuit, the inference being that as food for greyhounds, this new Spillers product would help your dogs win a lot. By the 1930s, the biscuits had become a brand leader, and eventually, they branched out into all types of dog foods and snacks.

With a history of growth through acquisition and mergers, the board clearly saw the value in owning the best kennels in the country. Sometimes, you have to look beyond the products you're selling to the wider brand association. After seeing this place, Spillers agreed to buy half the business, installing a shop where they could sell pet food, dog bones and collars. Pretty soon, they wanted to upgrade the kennels too, but their new partner said, "Look, you came to me because I was the best, but I don't have the money to do what you're picturing."

Now, Spillers may have wanted the brand association, but that didn't mean they wanted to be *in* the kennel business. Reluctantly, they bought out their partner and took control of the company. The question now was, 'How can we elevate this even further?' What they came up with was incredible.

When you arrived with your Cavalier King Charles Spaniel at the all-new Splillers' Kennels, the receptionists didn't talk to you; they spoke to the dog.

"Hey, Trixie, it's so nice to meet you," Anne says, crouching down on her haunches to accept a paw. "We've been expecting you. Are you excited for your holiday?"

The interaction immediately puts her owner at ease, and the guilt of leaving her dog for a week is already starting to fade. "She certainly is. We just need to finalise the details."

"Lovely," Anne replies. "How can we settle you in then, Trixie? Do you like having the TV on?"

"Oh, she loves a bit of *Coronation Street!*" her owner says.

"Do you want us to put that on every night, Trixie, so you recognise the music and don't miss Mummy whilst she's away?"

"Oh, that'd be lovely," the owner replies as the bill goes up by 50p a day.

"And how many walks do you expect? I bet you're a right little handful, aren't you?"

The owner's thinking about the one walk a day she takes Trixie on in the morning, but she doesn't want anyone else to know that. "Oh, two, or even three sometimes," she says.

"Well, we can walk you three times a day, no problem, Trixie. There's one already included, but you can add a walk for £2 a day!"

Before you know it, you've spent an extra £70 on all the add-ons, but you're over the moon because you can finally take a guilt-free holiday. You have access to the CCTV, so you can check in on Trixie whenever you want.

The whole experience reminded me of Trill. When I was young, almost every household had a budgie, and everyone who had a budgie bought their birdseed from Trill. Sooner or later, though, their growth began to plateau. If you're selling pet food, you're at the mercy of how many people actually own said pets.

Trill's response was to run an advert on TV that showed their awareness of the bigger picture. The ad didn't focus on how much your budgie loved Trill or how brilliant their business was; instead, they told you that it was cruel to have one budgie. If you couldn't spend hours with your bird every day, you needed to get another one, so they had some company. When the ad finished, we all slowly turned our heads. As Joey rocked back and forth on his swing, the cage bars became more sinister and that same posture he'd always had suddenly seemed sad and dejected. By the following week, Joey had a friend, and we'd doubled our birdseed order.

You might not have the budget to be the pinnacle of your industry, you might not even want to be, but what you can do is study what works for the biggest players. Collect any little nuggets of wisdom and apply them to your company – anything to keep your customers coming back.

Chapter 5

How to Exit a Business

For most new entrepreneurs, their vision of success in business is to build a company, sell it, and walk away from the deal financially free. When you reach that point, though, on the precipice of achieving your goal, it's not always as cut and dry as you'd think. You're saying goodbye to something you've birthed, raised and been to hell and back with. If you're anything like me, you may have invested more than half of your life into it. So, when it grows up, becomes self-sufficient and threatens to leave home, you're caught between clicking your heels and wondering how much of your identity will go with it.

On the eve of selling City Cruises, I almost pulled out. I wasn't just having second thoughts, I was having 40 years of thoughts all at once. What about our family legacy? The decades of hard graft? The hundreds of people who worked for me? Was I letting them all down?

For a little while there, I didn't care about the months of preparation, the promises I'd made to the buyer, or the shareholders. I just couldn't let go.

But the next morning, when I walked into our lawyer's offices to put the last signatures on the contract, I knew we were making the right decision. I just didn't have the years left. The Millennium Diamond was the last boat we built from scratch; it took seven years from the moment we started planning to the day passengers could climb aboard. If I wanted to build another, I'd have been in my mid-70s by the time it arrived. I started looking over my five and 10-year plans for the business, and then it hit me: When you start building for a future beyond your own sell-by date, you know it's time to think about succession.

My son wanted to be CEO, and he could have done a great job, but that doesn't mean it was best for him. Both our kids grew up in the business, sacrificing their holidays and even their mealtimes to hear about this staffing dilemma or that tax consideration. It took me a long time to realise that my needs were different from theirs. If I sold the company, it would give them more options; they could follow their own dreams.

I created City Cruises, sure, but just like my

children, it had outgrown me. The company that purchased it had the resources to take it global. It was time to let go.

One day you might take your business as far as your money, time, knowledge, ability, interest, health, or geography will allow. If and when that becomes the case, then get out; don't let it implode because of indecision. Just make sure you time it right. Ask yourself, 'Do I really want to sell?' Because once it's gone, there's no going back.

How to Value Your Business

When the dust has settled on the reindeers, mistletoe and *Die Hard* reruns, the start of a new year appears as a helpful reminder to value your business. For most industries, the first week of January will likely be a quieter period than usual, so why not make use of the time? If you have ambitions of selling one day, it's crucial to budget for an independent evaluator to come in, perhaps once a year, and assess the company.

It's about more than how much you made versus how much you spent. You need to understand where you sit in the marketplace, how much you've grown from the previous year, and what you can do to improve.

If you run a coffee shop and had 10,000 customers

last year, you have to figure out where your growth can come from. Can you physically fit any more people in your shop? Would you need to knock a wall down or open a new location? I remember when we first turned over a million passengers in a year. It wasn't as simple as 'get more customers', it was *when* could we get them. In the summer, we were full to the brim. The only way we could get more people on board was if we broke maritime law or got another boat. So, the question shifted from 'How can we let more people know we exist?' to 'How can we get more people to join us over the other nine months of the year?'

RULE OF THUMB

Highlight where
the growth
is happening.

An evaluator will help you know where to look. You get the report back and sit around with the shareholders and non-execs to discuss which way the line's moved. If your business was worth a million last year, perhaps you're aiming for at least a 5% growth. Whatever your target, you need *something* you can show to your stakeholders and the *lenders* who might be funding your next phase of expansion.

The deeper you dig, the more anomalies you'll find. We sold more cups of tea when our boats were half full. It blew our minds at first. How could that be? Two hundred extra people, almost half the revenue. At first, we thought it must be the queues; maybe people didn't want to stand in line for that long. But you can't guess. You need to speak to customers to understand their psychology.

"How was your journey today, madam?"

"Oh, it was wonderful, thank you, dear."

"Is there anything that would have made it better?"

"A cup of tea would have made my day!"

"We have plenty of tea at the bar. Did you get a chance to look?"

"Oooo no. I wouldn't want to lose my seat."

Can you hear that? That's the sound of a penny dropping. Of course. If you arrive early and get a window seat or a bench on the top deck, who'd want to give that up for a builder's tea?

So, when you get back to the boardroom, you're asking, "Does anyone have any ideas?" You throw a bunch of possibilities out. Maybe we need roaming waiting staff to take orders at the seats. Or perhaps we could put tea stations on both decks. How about we revisit Lonnie's playbook and introduce packages? Buy a tea and get two biscuits included or free refills for a family of four.

RULE OF THUMB

You must know
the numbers.

How much money have you got in the bank? What are the current stock levels? When was the last time you valued the stock? Last year it was worth £100,000, but this year it could be worth £110,000. An evaluator will help you to understand the numbers beneath the surface: what borrowing you have, what the interest rates are, and what's happening with inflation.

If you want to get the best value for your business, you need to sell at the right time. It's no good going to market when the growth has stopped; by then, you've left it too late. On the flip side, maybe you've valued the business three years in a row, and it keeps getting exponentially higher. If you continue following the plan, in five years, you could exit with an extra zero on the end.

Why would you sell now and let someone else cash in on your years of hard work? Well, probably because you didn't know any better. Without the right data, you're speeding along a winding road with your eyes closed, trying to guess where the next turning is. You can't make reasonable decisions without opening your field of vision and giving yourself time to process all the twists and turns.

One thing that will come out of a valuation is your EBITDA (Earnings Before Interest, Taxes, Depreciation and Amortisation), a commonly used metric to determine how much money a business makes from its core operations. EBITDA helps potential buyers compare businesses across industries without being muddied by each company's specific circumstances (like differing tax and interest rates).

If your company has an EBITDA of one million,

you can approach buyers with a multiple. For example, you might be selling at 5 x EBITDA, in which case, a potential buyer can say, "If we pay five million for this company, it will take us approximately five years to recoup our investment."

While EBITDA is a great measuring stick, it is still just a guide. There are many elements that can affect the multiple: Comparable acquisitions (especially from your industry), company specifics (like growth and competitive advantages), market conditions, and, of course, the big one – negotiation. If you want any chance of walking away feeling like you got a good deal, you must realise that none of this preparation matters without the story that goes with it.

RULE OF THUMB

To get the best deal, you need a better story.

You can show as many graphs and charts as you like, but you still need to sell the vision. Tell them about the new boat arriving next year that will double your capacity for evening tours and increase your standing in the marketplace. Highlight the big contracts you've won and the infrastructure changes that will cut costs and improve efficiency. Hand over your little book of acquisitions that pinpoints the competitors that could be ripe for the picking.

Like any sale, you're trying to enhance the great things about your business and show people how much better their lives will be after they've purchased it.

Stay Ready (So You Don't Need to Get Ready)

If the roles were reversed, would you buy your company? If the answer is no, it's probably because you know where the faults are. So, clean them up. Build some structure in your organisation. We've talked about how vital HR and infrastructure are. Look at your recruitment process, job descriptions, psychometric testing, health and safety, budgets, cash flow and insurance.

Think of it like any mature relationship. It doesn't matter how attractive you are, the more complicated you make it, the less likely people are to stick around.

When a potential buyer comes in, you should be able to hand them detailed records: a company handbook, training manuals, contracts, revenue forecasts, stock levels, cash flow and management accounts. You need to give them the confidence that if they took the keys tomorrow, they could steer the ship with or without you.

Speak to your accountant

Tell them you're thinking about selling. Ask them what you need to put together for potential buyers and get them to assess what you currently have and give you some critiques.

Lawyer up, buddy

Start speaking to law firms *before* you have a buyer. You don't want to rush into *any* business dealings if you can avoid it, but especially one so vital to your future.

Tell them what you're looking to do; they will undoubtedly bring up a dozen things you hadn't considered. You want the sale process to run as smoothly and as efficiently as possible; you have a buyer now, but they won't be around forever. Good lawyers can help you get the hard work done early *before* your buyer has a chance to change their mind.

All this preparation will help you answer almost any question with confidence, and to get your best price, confidence is crucial.

Ask yourself, is now the time to sell?

Once you've spoken to your accountant and the lawyers, they may advise against selling... yet. Perhaps the market conditions favour the buyer. Not everything is in your control, so you must be patient and understand that everything moves in cycles. Village wine bars might be sexy at the moment, whereas, for whatever reason, hotels just aren't flavour of the month. Maybe your assets will double in value if you hold on to them for another few years, or you might attract more interest by building a stronger management team and cutting overheads first.

On the other hand, you could have timed it just right. Your industry might be all over the news at the moment, or your products endorsed by a global celebrity. There are also tax and VAT timelines to consider. Your accountant may be pushing to get the deal done before the next HMRC payment comes out.

When we sold City Cruises, Hornblower made us an offer on day one. We didn't finish on this number, but it showed how serious they were and how keen they were to get into the London market. We soon had them set up in our office to work with our finance team. Once they'd started investing time and money into making the deal happen, we felt increasingly confident we could get it over the line.

Having said that, we weren't only talking to them; they were fully aware we had other parties interested (and if they ever forgot, I was sure to remind them). If you have one buyer, you're at their mercy. But if you can attract a handful of bidders, you can ensure that the numbers keep going in the right direction.

Sign a non-disclosure agreement
"If they don't buy, they don't buy! What's the worst thing that can happen?"

Well, you could wheel in the giant wooden horse, totally unaware that an army is inside it just waiting for you to go to sleep so it can climb down, attack your people and raze your city.

Okay, that's a bit dramatic, but let's look at the facts. You've let an outsider into your company, given them your business plan, laid out your infrastructure and finances, gone into detail about how you became successful, and discussed your strengths and weaknesses, only for them to decide, "Actually, we're fine, thanks. I've had a better idea!"

Whilst you can't force someone to buy your company, you have to try and mitigate the danger. A non-disclosure agreement (or NDA) prohibits all parties from sharing sensitive information. You may have sent these to suppliers or contractors before or been asked to sign them yourself. They're not watertight, but they will give you some recourse if someone does run off with your data.

You can also try to implement some financial safety nets. In some scenarios, you may be able to ask for a deposit, then, at least, you will walk away with something for your time if the deal falls through. Another option is to sell exclusivity for a short period. This will give the buyer time to review the details and remove some of your risk. As the deal progresses, though, sooner or later, they're going to have to spend their own money. They'll be paying their staff, accountants and lawyers, and the more time and money they commit, the more you can believe their intentions.

Host a beauty parade

"I wouldn't know who to sell to."

Thankfully, there are companies that exist to put buyers and sellers together within a certain price range. So, if your turnover is £25 million, you might find an expert who helps sell businesses with revenues from £15–£30 million. It's their job to find the types of entities who might want to purchase you.

Assuming what you have is attractive enough to buy, you might even have too many. It will serve you well to quickly whittle them down to a handful that you can have longer, meaningful discussions with.

It's easy to think you'll just go with the highest bidder, but it doesn't always work like that. When we bought Gillingham Marina, we were competing with property developers who had an endless pit of resources. But, thankfully for us, the Marina was a family-run business and ultimately, the board chose us because of our commitment to their vision. In other words, we wouldn't just level everything and build a block of flats. They knew we'd look after the current staff and honour the suppliers' contracts and client events.

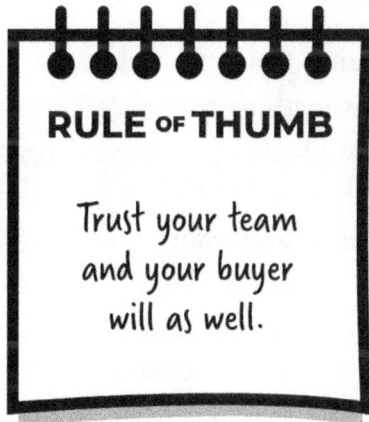

RULE OF THUMB

Trust your team
and your buyer
will as well.

When we sold City Cruises in 2019, it was much the same. I'd spent a lifetime building that business; I didn't want to see it stripped and sold for parts. We knew Hornblower would look after our people, from casual staff to directors and consultants.

While agents will work hard to find you buyers, you do have to be careful. Have a think about how they're paid. You want to structure their fee so it's in their interest to get you the best deal. You may think that the commission on the back end will do the trick, but there's an old saying: Points on the board are better than a game in hand. If an agent can guarantee a deal, they will likely rush it through rather than risk losing it all. In the same way, if you have a beauty parade for your business, make sure you speak to several agents until you find one you can work with.

Figure out what's driving the buyers

You can't leave anything to chance. The more you can find out about your buyer's intentions, the easier a deal will be for both of you. Do they want to enter a new market, take over your patents or just increase their assets? They could be trying to reduce their tax liability by investing in other businesses, in which case, they may pay over the odds. If you know they're seeking an aggressive expansion, produce a growth document that shows where the market is heading.

Highlight possible future acquisitions in the industry. Show them a clear path for the future.

It's like any deal; you must consider what is good for both sides. Whatever happens, always be 100% helpful to new bidders. They can walk away if you're rude or arrogant, even if you think they won't. There are plenty of other companies out there.

Take a week off!

Throw your phone off Waterloo Pier, put your *out of office* on and go and sit on a beach.

"Are you crazy?" I hear you say. "All hell would break loose. I'm trying to sell my company, not bankrupt myself this close to the finish line."

If you can't leave your office for fear of what might (or might not) happen in your absence, you're probably not ready to sell. If you can remove yourself from the equation, the new owners will have a plug-and-play business that they can take in any direction they want. Think how much more they'll be willing to pay for that. If you need to be there, you either haven't trained your people correctly or you are too attached to the role; either way, you don't have the right processes in place.

When I sold City Cruises, I forwarded every email from the buyer to someone else in the team. I didn't want them to rely on me for *anything*.

Put yourself in the buyer's position. What would you want? An owner-free business that you can mould to fit in with the bigger vision, or someone in the boardroom saying, "But we've always done it this way." How will that person make unbiased decisions when you've come in and taken over something they've poured so much of their soul into? Suddenly, you have divided loyalties; a senior management team caught between 'the processes that got them here' and the new way of thinking.

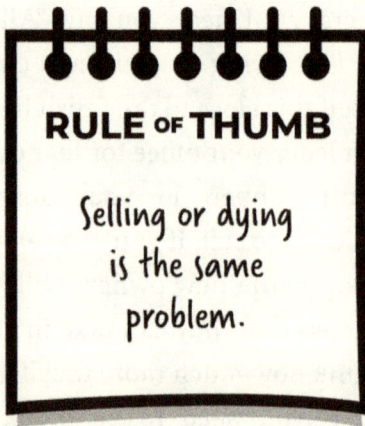

RULE OF THUMB

Selling or dying
is the same
problem.

As strange as this sounds, you have to make sure you're NOT an asset as quickly as possible. The business must survive without you.

If you own a barbershop, it's unlikely you can stop

cutting hair on day one. But as the word gets out, hopefully, you'll fill up another three chairs. Of course, three staff won't be enough, because you'll all need holidays, later starts and sick days. So, gradually, you move from cutting hair to managing barbers. You purchase another site and focus more on building the brand than working in the shop.

I must stress there's nothing wrong with cutting hair if that's what you love to do. You can make yourself a great life working for yourself. But if you want to maximise your sale price, you must transition to a place where, if you never used a pair of clippers again, the business still runs. Work through all the areas the business needs until you can either employ someone to take over (or until you can outsource the role). Then, get yourself into a non-exec position as quickly as possible.

Hire non-executive directors

An executive role means you're there five days a week, working in the business as well as making decisions. Non-executives might come in once a month or once a week. They will help the board take decisive action on policy, business direction, or investments. It's their job to provide their expertise to help the company do what's best. They'll ask the right questions: What's our skill base? What are we good at? Are we moving too far away from that with this new venture? How risky is the client? Should we be putting all our eggs in one basket? Why are we buying new assets with cash flow? Is there a better way? Should we lease or buy the freehold? Freehold uses up cash, but in five years, it might make us more attractive to buyers.

A non-exec will maximise advice, minimise risk and always have an eye on profit. Pro-rata, they'll be the highest-paid people in the business, but you won't have to pay them an arm and a leg because you may only need them twice a month. You don't have to worry about finding them work to do; you just wheel them in when you need their help.

It's their job to run through these scenarios with you. They're unlikely to be career-minded, so they're just going to do their job. They're not looking over their shoulder like they might do in corporate life, worrying about who's trying to usurp their position or steal their ideas. They just read the minutes, sit down for a leisurely meeting, and tell you what they know.

Succession Planning

Everything we've covered so far in this section can be filed under 'succession planning'.

> ## RULE OF THUMB
>
> Plan for success
> with succession
> planning.

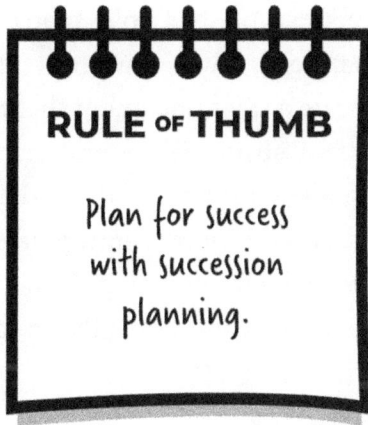

People buy well-run, owner-free, solid companies, especially if they see organic growth. They want to know they can take your business and run with it without spending months waiting for you to get your act together. The best way to get to this point is to plan for what happens after you depart (the business or the world).

In theory, business is simple. Proceed to Go. Collect your £200. Pay the tax. Stay out of jail. Buy property. Find a banker you can trust. Take chances. Give back to the community and always celebrate free parking.

I guess the lesson is to never stray too far from the simple things. When you're planning for the future, be sure to take advice at every stage. Speak to your accountant, lawyers and consultants. Hire a non-executive director who has sold many companies. Enter competitions, win awards, build your reputation. Create a sales document that includes PR, social media, the website, a sales and marketing plan, training manuals and finances. Work with trade bodies, mentors and other entrepreneurs. Go to business clubs and keep learning. Don't cut corners. And plan like your future depends on it, because it really does.

You've Made Your Money... Now what?

In late 2019, after 40 years building our empire, we sold City Cruises. I'm always reticent to use the word 'luck', but there's no denying that timing was on our side. Somehow, we'd circumnavigated a global pandemic, and we could spend the majority of 2020 strategising our next steps.

Over the years, we'd reached heights we'd never dreamed of. We'd created a business that employed over 500 people, set sail with the Queen on board, entertained the future king, prime ministers and celebrities, lobbied with the government, won contracts for the Millennium Dome and the 2012 Olympic Games, and spent tens of millions building our own vessels. The crowning achievement was perhaps Rita receiving an OBE for her services to the leisure and tourism industry and the regeneration of London's Docklands.

However, once we'd finally made our money, none of that seemed to matter. It was as if we were starting all over again as beginners in a strange new world. Every day, we'd hear unfamiliar words stacked on top of terms we didn't understand. It was like learning a new language, but one that was structured entirely in financial jargon.

It's not like you have to do it all by yourself; finding help is no longer the problem. The minute you put the pound sign up, you'll never be short of advice. Everyone will have ideas regarding what you can do with your money. You'll start to wonder, *Can I trust this person? Do I need a second opinion? Do I need a third?*

The reality is you can't just follow what other people are telling you; you must gain a fundamental understanding of finance yourself before making any decisions, and every decision involves taxation and legislation. So, you become an armchair tax expert. You buy Premium Bonds and pay money into your ISA. You max out your pensions and figure out your life insurance. You get on top of it. Then the government announces a Mini-Budget, and everything changes again.

When you sail past retirement age, if you can afford to, you'll likely want to stop working. Maybe you want to spend more time with the grandkids, or you can finally afford that world cruise. But, for most people, I think they stop working because their bodies have. At 70 years old, your knees can sound like the creaking floorboards of a haunted townhouse, your hips have less movement than a monk's morning routine, and your back feels like you've carried the weight of every wrong decision you've ever made. Then you go to a dinner party with old friends, the majority of whom have all but given up battling their weight. We're on painkillers for our ailments, statins for our cholesterol and a concoction of tablets that would put most Glastonbury crowds to shame. Not to mention that no one is getting any sleep because we're visiting the toilet 10 times a night.

Why would you even contemplate going back to work? For some, it's a financial necessity; for others, it's the only thing that gets them out of bed in the morning. But for us, it was about family. Our focus shifted to putting our loved ones in the strongest financial position possible.

In truth, there's no such thing as 'never having to work again'. One way or another, you'll have to put your money to work. After decades of sacrifice and risk, you might be too old to enjoy all the benefits the money finally brings you, but it's nice to think you can pass all those opportunities to your loved ones, so long as you don't fall at the final hurdle.

Anything we have above the government's inheritance threshold (currently at £325,000) is taxed at 40% before it's bequeathed to our beneficiaries. When you know this, money becomes its own scorecard, and the game is to move cash out of your estate and into anything that will allow you to pass on the most wealth to your family. If I die tomorrow, I want to leave my kids and grandkids as much as I can, whether it's in cash, assets or stocks and shares. You must understand the rules and work them to your advantage, or you risk losing up to 40% of what you've spent a lifetime working for.

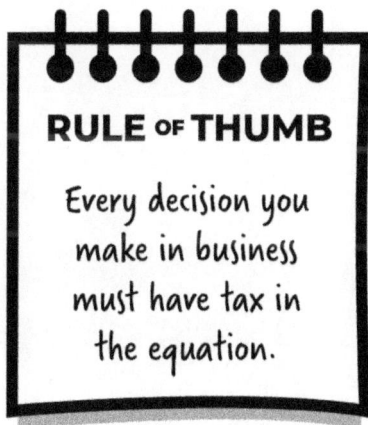

RULE OF THUMB

Every decision you make in business must have tax in the equation.

I remember sitting with Rita after we'd sold City Cruises. As we combed through all our accounts, interest rates and tax liabilities, the reality of what we had to do dawned on me. I turned to her and said, "Well, it looks like we're back in business."

Chapter 6

How to Buy a Business

After selling the company I'd nurtured for over 40 years, I was at a loss over what to do next.

Perhaps I should have been clicking my heels every morning, dancing the Hula on my way to the beach. I just couldn't shake the feeling that I shouldn't have done it, that I'd given away our family legacy. Within a few months, though, the pandemic came crashing down on us all, and the timing of the deal looked like a stroke of genius.

By the time COVID-19 was in full swing, my concerns had shifted from what I'd done to what we should do next. We were experts in running boats, but now we were running money, and that was an entirely different beast. With my age and energy levels always a consideration, I warmed to opportunities that weren't too labour intensive, places where I could invest cash and help guide the vision and the infrastructure without running the day-to-day operations.

My first thought was storage. Why not buy a container for £5,000 and rent it out for £200 per month? We could start small and grow it based on demand; every time we filled one up, we could buy another. We could easily have 10 containers and a nice little business running in no time. Once we got to a certain size, we could purchase some cheap real estate and operate from our own location. Apart from the cost of the containers and somewhere to put them, we'd have very few overheads. It was a simple model, and it meant I wouldn't have to be on-site every day.

However big, small, good or bad you think your ideas are at first, you must treat them all the same, flesh them out and see where they end up. Ideas can shift and change shape until they barely resemble their original selves, but they also create a network that leads to other options, like the London Tube Map connecting distant stations.

We began investigating warehouses around 10,000 square feet. If we took over spaces that already had a tenant in-situ, we'd know the numbers we were walking into and could show the bank our forecast based on realistic returns. We were so serious about it that we expanded our search. This business wouldn't operate in a vacuum, so we investigated smaller and larger sites so we could assess the market as a whole. Then we switched locations. If we were to buy an acre of land in Dover, it might be worth £2.5 million, but if we wanted a similar space in, let's say, Tunbridge Wells, it could be £8 million more.

You're always trying to land on a sweet spot: a good location but at an affordable price. It sounds obvious, but you'd be surprised by how many people don't use all the information at their disposal.

RULE OF THUMB

Have a rule
of thumb.

They see a good site or a cheap price and convince themselves it will work. You can't operate entirely on gut instinct; there needs to be some logic thrown in there, too. Your gut only comes into play when you've taken in all the information you can, and you're trying to make a tough decision; it shouldn't be at the expense of facts. If in doubt, you need to be guided by basic business principles.

Allow your risks to be taken on a foundation of logic. Our guiding star was simple: How much will we spend per square foot versus how much can we sell it for? We do the research, and we pop the numbers into a model and see what it spits out. If we have two equally compelling locations with similar revenue and profit and not much to choose between them, maybe now we're using our gut. Which one feels right? Where do we envision ourselves in a few years if we pick this site over the other? Which landlord did we have a better connection with?

While you're investigating potential industries to dive into, it's just as important to know which ones to avoid. The quicker you can rule things out, the more direct your route to success. For instance, we'd owned several restaurants and bars, but in 2021, the future of hospitality was looking bleak, so in the short term at least, we weren't considering them.

You can't account for everything. Some things will be out of your control, and as a founder, you learn to accept that. You realise you can utilise all the info at your disposal and follow your gut at the right times, but there's still a little thing called luck that will show up out of nowhere.

Our warehouse business was one interruption away from becoming a reality. I was sitting in my living room, sipping on a tea and having one last comb through the contract when my son-in-law, Aaron, burst into the room.

"I think I've found it!" he said.

"Oh, great!" I replied without looking up. "Maybe you can buy a round at last."

Aaron paused. "Not my wallet! A site. The perfect site."

I looked up at him and then back down at the lease for our new warehouse. "Alright," I said, tossing it onto the table. "Show me what you've got."

* * *

The business began as a small automotive dealership just after the Second World War, but like any idea that's been allowed to breathe, it no longer resembled its original form. The location backed onto the River Medway, and due to its proximity to the water, owners Leonard and Eric Parham thought it prudent to add Yacht Repair to their services in the 1950s.

In the '60s, they acquired a neighbouring

company – Alan's Boat Yard – as Mr Alan was looking to retire, and they expanded across the site. By the time we arrived for our first recce in 2021, Gillingham Marina was 19.2 acres of waterfront possibility, a multi-facility operation spanning many industries, from marine and maritime to hospitality, and health and leisure.

Despite decades of success, the business had been losing money in recent years, and the board's appetite to solve the next problem had dwindled, opening the doors for one family business to hand over the keys to another.

As we wandered around, taking it all in, I knew I'd have three big questions to answer when I got back home. Anytime you're looking to buy a new business, you must know this first:

1. How much money do I need to purchase the site and have someone manage it for me?
2. How much money can I make?
3. What is the risk?

These three questions are almost universal, regardless of the industry or product.

Once you're satisfied with all those answers – and before you can even consider a deal – you still have to think about your exit. Give yourself a Jason Bourne moment: You don't want to get into something if you don't have a way out. If the worst happened and we couldn't make the business profitable, we could always sell the land. That doesn't mean it was risk free; if the sale was delayed for any reason, we could start haemorrhaging money.

RULE OF THUMB

Get more opinions.

Over the next few months, I went back and forth to the marina, going in and out like the changing tide and showing all kinds of people the opportunity. I invited our bank managers, accountants and business friends. I spoke to hospitality titans, fitness gurus and real-estate moguls. We brought in potential partners that might joint venture on certain areas and investors that could one day be our exit.

When you're considering spending large amounts of time and money on big projects, you must allow the people you trust to help you make the decision.

Normally, if your business plan is solid enough, a bank might say, "We'll give you 80% of what you need; you have to come up with the other 20%." That's what I was expecting. But after showing them our strategy for Gillingham Marina, they said, "This is fantastic, we'll give you the lot."

Our accountant doubled down, saying, "I actually can't see a downside!"

So, in December 2021, after months of negotiations, we became the proud owners of Gillingham Marina. The site had five key areas: the marina, which at the time berthed around 270 boats, maintenance and repairs, the Chandlery, a shop selling useful parts for the vessels, a gymnasium, and a waterfront bar and restaurant.

Despite the size of the business and the various elements, objectively, there were very few moving parts, at least compared to City Cruises. Back then, we had offices all over London, as well as in York and Poole. We had 500 staff and 40 vessels. The sales team were in and out all day, and so were the boats. With the marina, though, everything was in one place. It was an incredible opportunity for us. We knew the industry, we had the passion and energy to turn things around, and we had the foresight to plan for the worst and work for the best.

Best Laid Plans

Before buying a company, you have to think about your exit. Ask yourself: If my business plan doesn't work, what other options do I have?

Before we bought Gillingham Marina, we were in a strong position because most people don't understand boats. There's a learning curve with any new industry, but I guess figuring out the tides and maritime legislation puts people off about as much as the cold winter mornings and the thought of always being a bit damp.

Our competition to buy the business, therefore, perhaps unsurprisingly, was mostly property developers. It doesn't take much shipping knowledge to knock down obstacles and build flats for rich people. If these guys were serious about buying, ultimately, there was very little we could do; they could outbid us 10 times over.

Sometimes, though (and I do mean sometimes), money isn't everything. When you bulldoze over a site like this, you're destroying almost a century of family history with it. I knew the board wouldn't want to see everything they'd built broken to pieces. The question was, what was more important to them, the money or the history?

I was confident they would fall on the side of history because A) I'd spoken to them and B) I'd already gone through it. When I sold City Cruises, I picked the people that I thought could build on the legacy, not those who would dismantle it and sell it for parts. I wanted to ensure my loyal staff still had jobs and worked for people who could help them grow. The Gillingham Marina board felt the same. They knew we'd come in, put our arms around their team, listen to them, and support their transition.

The former owners struggled to turn the business around after the pandemic, but that didn't mean they didn't care about what happened to everyone who still worked there. Selling to us allowed them to cash in and be safe in the knowledge that a team of experts would look after their people and take their history forward.

Now, in retrospect, all of that's an interesting part of the story, but it's how we used the information at the time that really matters. If you want the best price for anything (whether you're buying or selling), you need to be willing to walk away if the deal's not right. I knew they wouldn't want to sell to property developers, so I found a reasonable price and stuck to it. If they wanted to take more money somewhere else, then so be it. But I had a gut feeling that we were the only ones that could give them what they wanted.

If, for whatever reason, we couldn't make the business work, the property developers would still be there. We wouldn't be trapped because we'd have an incredible asset that people would want. That's a backup plan.

My daughter, Lucy, creates high-end music festivals, so we ran the numbers. If we couldn't get the gym running or the Chandlery lost money, how much would it cost to build the infrastructure for live music instead? Was it feasible to erect a perimeter wall, have onsite sewage, and more toilets? If you wanted to sell tickets and put on a show, how great would it be not to have to worry about storage, CCTV, walk-in fridges, and where you can put the security offices? What if we'd already built it all for you? And what if you had a backdrop of the River Medway?

Before we signed anything, we had hundreds of conversations about what we could do there, many of which had absolutely nothing to do with the current structure. We have every intention of building from what's already there and helping it thrive and grow. We have zero intention of not being able to pay back the bank. That's why we have backup plans.

No matter how strong your plan B is, how good your intel, or how in tune you are with your gut, purchasing a business is always a risk, especially one that's losing money. We had to make quick decisions and take fast action.

Sure, we had five-year and 10-year plans, but our immediate focus was: How can we get more revenue through the door? What can we do *right now* to get the line going the right way? Thankfully, we had a tried and tested blueprint.

RULE OF THUMB

There are four ways to grow your business.

Chapter 7

How to Grow a Business

There are Four Ways to Grow Your Business:

1. Get new business (of the type you want)
2. Get your customers to come back
3. Get your customers to spend more money
4. Improve your processes

These four areas can be addressed by any business of any size. It doesn't matter how much you have in the budget; if you're not winning customers, keeping them, finding ways for them to spend more with you, and implementing processes all the way along, you're probably struggling right now. Let's investigate each area a little deeper.

Get new business (of the type you want)
The customer *isn't* always right!

Winning new business is only half the answer; it must be the *right* business. If you have a client who treats you poorly, offers less than your asking price and always pays late, give yourself permission not to work with them in the future. The time and energy that's drained from your soul in these relationships will be much better served if it's poured into finding people you enjoy working with and who pay you what you're worth.

It's just as crucial to know the types of clients you *don't* want as the ones you do. There's no point advertising to people who can't afford your product. If you're running a luxury hotel, you wouldn't hand out flyers at Freshers' Week. Even if the students could afford it, do your older guests (who make up the bulk of your customers) want to be surrounded by youngsters who bring a wildly different energy to your restaurants, bars and spas? You've been marketing "An oasis away from the hustle and bustle of the city", and instead you've got impromptu karaoke and communal vomiting.

It's not about alienating groups or turning people away; it's about understanding who your core audience is and talking directly to them. At Gillingham Marina, we're looking for clients with more than just a passing interest in boats. Our messaging is aimed at people who own one or who might look to buy, sell, clean, upgrade or go for a sail on one at least semi-regularly. Maybe their friends have boats, too.

In general, these kinds of people may have gone through the cycle of life – work, kids – and perhaps now they're close to retirement. Their outgoings are less than ever; they've had their mortgage for 30 years, their children have grown up, and there's a bit more cash to spend.

Once you've collected even a small amount of information, you can put a compass on a map and draw an arc around your business. For us, everyone fitting that description within a 60-mile radius of our site is a potential customer. Once identified, now all that's left is to give them a name!

John lives within 30 miles of us. He's just shy of 50 and married his wife Mary in his mid-20s. They own a beautiful home together. Mary loves a walk and John loves to keep Mary happy. Their kids are at university; they have two practical cars and a modest boat that's berthed at our marina.

When you know your customers' names, where they're from, and what their hobbies are, it makes it much easier to find more of them. Perhaps you do the research and notice that 90% of your revenue comes from people living in Greater London. You realise there's no need to cast a wider net; all you're doing is watering down your success rate.

If we have something to say, we're not cruising the streets on roller skates shouting our latest offers to anyone within range of a megaphone – we're talking directly to John and Mary. When we send out a mailer, we target their interests; we've got walking routes and seasonal menus, gift vouchers for the spa, talks by Olympic sailors or maritime experts and 20% off the Chandlery in May. You don't need to be a marketing guru to win new business. You only need to be experts in communicating with *your* John and Mary, and any other customer profiles that fit your business model.

Get your customers to come back
If only we owned trains. We could turn up when we wanted, charge a fortune and deliver a service so poor that a day without delays makes the customer feel like a luxury travel blogger.

"Where are you heading today, Sir?"

"Just off to King's Cross and then into the West End, please."

"Great. That'll be an extortionate price, please!"

"No problem," I say, smiling as I scan my debit card.

"Thank you, Mr Beckwith. Enjoy your journey!"

she says, handing me my ticket and breaking into a fit of super-villain laughter that I can still hear when I get to the platform.

The train pulls up, and the doors scrape open. One person steps off, 20 pile on. I'm in a hurry, so I decide to do it, stepping into the last bit of space (if you can call it that). I take a deep breath, and the door slams shut, almost catching my nose like a carrot on a chopping board. As I jostle for position, my cheek is smooshed against the steamy window, and I feel the jagged point of an elbow digging into my back. I notice an empty seat just by the aisle, but it's too far away and so filthy no one wants to sit on it. At the very end of the carriage, there's the blinking promise of a toilet light that I know I'll never reach. When I finally arrive at my destination, I'm seriously contemplating getting a taxi home that night, but a few hours later, there I am doing it all over again.

There are likely several people reading this who've been doing the same for decades. When faced with no other choice, it's amazing what we'll put up with.

In reality, though, unless your business has a monopoly, it is very unlikely anyone will settle for this kind of service. People seldom change their doctor or dentist, but for most industries, the competition is fierce and the customers fickle. If you want your clients to return, you have to earn it, and to do that, you must keep innovating.

Our old friend Lonnie knew that lawnmowers alone wouldn't attract people back to his shop, at least not in the same decade. He increased his floor space, expanded his product list, and made people feel special, remembering their names and sending them gift cards on their birthdays. On a sunny day, his customers would swing by for a cup of tea and a chat and, no doubt, pick up some more plants they didn't even need. Visiting Lonnie's became 'something to do' for his customers – an activity, not a task. Perhaps that's why they kept going back.

At the marina, we're constantly brainstorming ways to unite all the on-site operations and convince customers to spend more time there.

The gym works on a subscription model, so we're likely to see most of those clients return, as well as receive a regular income, but that's finite – they don't *have to* stay. It's our job to give them enough reasons to keep renewing their contracts. For some businesses, they might achieve this just by being the cheapest, but we want to offer things they can't get anywhere else. We put a lot of emphasis on our facilities; we've got ample parking, a café on site, incredible views of the River Medway, a spa with a steam room and sauna, racket sports, a swimming pool, basketball, hockey, five-a-side football courts, a snooker table, and a dance studio with spin classes.

Having so much to offer on one site is not only exciting for our guests, it's convenient. Our boat owners have access to a chandlery, so we don't have to send them off on an expedition every time their vessels need a service. While the work's being done, they can meet up with their friends in the bar or get a few miles in on the treadmill.

Perhaps a customer likes to train every Monday, Wednesday and Thursday, but at the weekend, they want to bring the kids down for some tennis or a swim. We'll regularly offer members one-on-one coaching, trial classes, discounts for the spa and complimentary guest passes to tempt them into exploring more of our services. We're always hoping they will try new things and meet new people, because if they do, they'll likely have a great experience, tell their friends and, ultimately, keep coming back.

Get your customers to spend more money

So, you've won new customers and convinced them to come and see you again. Now what? How can you get them to *spend* more? Well, why not learn from the best? You can say what you like about fast food, but McDonald's are masters of the upsell...

You're in a busy queue. It's 1am, and the booze is turning to sweat that's pouring from your temples.

"Would you like to make that a meal?" she says.

Well, you think, *I did promise myself just a cheeseburger, but...*

"Yes, please," you say before you've even finished the thought.

The young lady smiles like she already knew the answer. "And would you like to go large for an extra 80p?"

Her finger hovers ominously over the till.

80p, you think. You look up at the board. Then you hear a bleep.

"That'll be £7.79, please," she says.

Wait. What happened? Did I say yes? Did I nod? How did she know?

You pay your money and take your food. By the first handful of fries, you're convinced that 'going large' was the best decision you've ever made.

When Lonnie first started his lawnmower business, he spent many a night ordering fast food on the way home, unable to face a couple more hours on his feet cooking a healthy dinner. As he was eating out one night, he spotted a guy alone in the packed restaurant, nodding to his headphones and unwrapping a solitary beef burger – no chips, no drinks, just a burger. Lonnie swivelled his head. One guy with one burger. Every other person on every other table had a meal – every single one. The penny dropped.

Lonnie took out his phone and started writing down packages. Instead of selling a plant, he'd have a deal that came with the pot, some soil and some gardening gloves. He realised he'd make less money on the individual products, but – he looked around – if he priced it just right, he'd shift more units and make a killing.

Lonnie's packages became so popular that his average spend per customer went up by almost 20%. And he didn't stop there. He emailed people with offers to tempt them in during his quiet months. He sent video tutorials on how to grow specific flowers, stop pigeons nicking all the bird seed, and 'How to clean out your pond without wiping out the pond life.'

Rather than spending all his time worrying about how much revenue he was bringing in, he focused on increasing his average spend per customer. Before long, he could work out exactly how many people he needed to get through the door to achieve his financial goals. He could give tangible figures to the bank and investors to borrow against growth and refine his offerings to test what sent the numbers in the right direction.

At the marina, our customers pay to moor their boats, but they also need electricity for their generators. At least once a year, they'll lift their ships out of the water to survey it; maybe they need to update their anodes, inspect their bearings, get a paint job or have someone assess their propellers. Sometimes, they might just want a deep clean. By offering more than just a place to park, we're generating extra revenue and giving our guests a reason to stay a little longer.

Improve your processes

If you've read this far, you'll already know how I feel about processes. From Derrick's drill bits and Lonnie's Lawnmowers to acclimatisation rotas, job descriptions, health and safety and hiring, if this book could be boiled down to one word, *'processes'* might well be it. Everything needs to be written down and communicated. If you make a commitment to building the right infrastructure from the beginning, it will transform your company's future. You will operate more efficiently, save time and money, and make yourself much more attractive to top talent, high-paying clients and potential buyers.

There's an old saying about Henry Ford that sums it up nicely: *Before he introduced automation, 12 people made one car. After automation, one person made 12 cars.*

Get the processes right, and, to a degree, the rest will build itself.

RULE OF **THUMB**

Processes are a
friend to business.

All four of the above strategies have been crucial to our success. At City Cruises, we understood early on who we were trying to attract. We were a family-run business with an approachable image, often hosting four generations of the same family for trips along the river. When we sent out communications, *that* was the audience we spoke to.

We diversified our products, which allowed our customers to return and try something new. They could come for sightseeing, afternoon tea, a dinner dance with entertainment, speed boat tours, or even charter a vessel for a private party. Our performers on 'The Show Boat' became so popular that people would come back with a new group of friends over and over again.

We also got them spending more. Instead of selling a ticket for a show, we wrapped it all up in a package. For £99 per person, you got a window seat, a five-course dinner, a champagne upgrade, entertainment and drinks. During the day, we partnered with tour operators and sold destination trips to places like the Cutty Sark, Greenwich and the Thames Barrier. We had merchandise available and incentives to book our other products.

Despite our understanding of all these areas, though, what really accelerated our growth was buying other companies. You see, technically, there are *six ways* to grow your business, but not everyone will have either the finances or the inclination required for *acquisitions* and *mergers*.

Acquisitions

When I started on the River Thames in the late 1970s, we purchased a dilapidated fuel barge. Our customers could sail over to us, fill up with diesel and head out for the day. The business was ticking along nicely until one morning, on the way to work, I stopped to get some petrol. As I approached the cashier, I nonchalantly grabbed a drink and a few snacks. It wasn't until I threw them on the passenger seat and watched my fizzy drink roll off into the footwell that I spotted what we were missing. We'd already done the hard part: the customers were coming to us, so why not offer them more? If you're out on the river all day, what if you run out of toilet roll or bottled water? I drove out of the petrol station determined to create London's first floating 'Cash & Carry'.

Before long, we had the customers coming back, and we had them spending more, but the problem was there just wasn't enough money on the river in those days, so a fuel barge was never going to make us rich, no matter how many cigarettes or long-life beers we could shift. It was time for acquisitions.

Our first purchase was The King, a Little Ship of Dunkirk with a capacity of 149 passengers. Overnight, we had access to a whole new customer base. We could offer sightseeing trips and private charters, squeezing every available minute from our new asset. As the revenue increased, though, we faced another problem. The King was 'open deck'. If we wanted to offer customers a more comfortable trip, we needed a boat with a roof. We bought the Eltham, with a capacity of 200 guests.

Over the years, these purchases became about much more than the assets; there was always a wider strategy. When we needed shore access, we bought the RS Hispaniola, which was permanently moored on the Embankment. We wanted more control over the sightseeing operations on the river, so we gradually bought out every company across two consortiums.

Sometimes, acquisitions gave us the size and types of vessels we were lacking, or maybe we didn't really need the boats, but they had a large customer base, fantastic office space, or a pier where we could store our fleet. There have been a few times when we bought a company, sold the boats we didn't need and effectively got the business for free.

It's not that we didn't want to build our own ships to grow the operation, but every time we bought something, it was akin to fast-forwarding our progress a few years. It was like a cheat code.

Still, for a long time, I held on to the dream of designing boats from scratch. Instead of shaping our business around a 100-year-old idea of what a boat should be, we could turn it on its head and start with the customer experience in mind. We could apply all our knowledge about what worked and what didn't and solve so many problems along the way.

We did achieve these goals eventually, several times in fact, but every time we built a new ship, the process took seven years and cost around seven figures. In the early days, not only did we lack the money or the knowledge, but we just couldn't wait that long.

I know what you're thinking: *It's all very well talking about acquisitions, but you must have had an angel investor, family money, or a sympathetic bank manager. We can't all be Hungry Hippos gobbling up any company we like the look of; we don't have the finances for that.*

I hear you because I was in *exactly* the same position. No sugar daddy, no family money (I grew up on a council estate in Leyton), and for my first 20 years in business, no bank would come anywhere near us. In fact, I'll go ahead and assume, in most cases, I was in a worse position than many people reading this. I got myself into a cottage industry that was falling apart from decades of stagnation. Even the keenest of gamblers wouldn't have backed us.

Our secret was to parlay our small wins into the next opportunity. We reinvested every penny back into the business. It meant taking some huge risks, but they were always calculated. If we weren't growing, we were withering away, so no matter what, we were gambling with the future (you can read about our acquisition strategy in-depth in the first book in this series). For now, that's enough of the 'how', here's a reminder of the 'why'.

RULE OF THUMB

The environment of a business will often dictate how large it can grow.

We became a big player in the UK, but we were always battling with geography. The Thames has restrictions on the size of vessels it will allow; there are also only two directions we could travel (upstream or downstream). By 2013, we were carrying millions of passengers a year; we'd hosted the Queen, prime ministers, global brands and celebrities, and we'd been involved in the Diamond Jubilee celebrations and providing transport for the Millennium Dome. Our sales team was the best in the business, but the problem was we were running out of things to sell. We knew we needed to expand beyond the confines of the river and set our sights on taking the brand outside London.

We purchased a small pleasure boat company operating from Poole Harbour in Dorset. On this occasion, taking over the business was more of a biproduct; the real value was in owning their boat and having access to the quay. With this new venture, our passengers could take a trip through Europe's largest natural harbour and the eastern tip of the Jurassic Coast. As per our growth strategy, we wanted more cash from each customer, so we added two more boats, a café and a road train styled like a miniature steam locomotive. We even brought our dinner dance concept over from London. In a very short time, we had the right clients returning and spending more with us.

Three years later, we found another site in York, which gave us a solid foothold up north. We weren't just buying companies on a whim; everything fed back into the long-term vision. Even after we sold City Cruises, I still never lost this mindset.

I knew I couldn't start a new company; I just didn't have the years left. But I needed to do *something*. Otherwise, when I pass on, where would all the money go? Who wants to work for 60 years and not be able to give the rewards to their family? For me, the only answer was what I'd been doing all my life: acquisitions. We now have dozens of business interests across many industries, diversifying our risk and maximising our estate.

Mergers

I still often wonder where I'd be now had we never sold. We didn't have the resources to grow City Cruises internationally the way Hornblower could, so I think mergers might have been the next step. Imagine if City Cruises had merged with Thames Clippers, for instance. When the O2 Arena chucks out 20,000 people on a Saturday night, we could send the whole fleet. The capacity and frequency would be mind blowing.

Joint marketing, fast boats, slow boats, small boats, big boats, a mammoth HR department, an unparalleled training school for captains, and eight million passengers a year. Of course, it's not all profits and sunshine. We'd have to think about merging the two cultures, staff rationalisation and whether regulatory bodies would try to block the deal from even happening.

When P&O merged with Carnival in 2003, they suddenly had two managing directors. As outsiders looking in, we knew this could be good for us; there would be a lot of uncertainty amongst the top talent at the company. By this point, I was obsessed with building infrastructure that would get us in a position to exit one day. Who better to hire than Gwyn Hughes, a former MD of P&O and one of the people instrumental in their merger with Carnival? We snapped up Gwyn, who became a non-executive director and a key component in our growth. Unfortunately, he passed away in 2013, but the foundations he helped to build over a decade set us up for our sale to Hornblower six years later.

Fast forward to present day. We own several companies, and thankfully, I'm no longer involved in the day-to-day operations. But whatever we buy and wherever we invest, we always bring the same blueprint that has worked for us time and time again, and an invaluable part of that is the four ways to grow your business.

The Dentist Theory

Neil's a dentist. He's young and ambitious, so he has no problem working long hours to build his reputation and get new customers. Everybody needs a dentist, so he soon figures out that he could work 10 hours a day, seven days a week if he wanted to. It's his practice, so the more he works, the more he earns. And that's precisely what he does.

What Neil doesn't realise just yet is that even for a young person at the beginning of his career, he's going to need a break at some point. You can't give your best self to your customers if you're too tired to interact with them. In some professions, you may be able to ride out your hangover with a brave face and a

Starbucks loyalty card, but when you're drilling inside people's mouths, steady hands and a clear head are perhaps the minimum that's expected each day. Besides, what's the point of earning all that money if you don't have time to spend it? Eventually, Neil's going to want a holiday, to have some time off sick, or to attend a family wedding.

So, what can he do? He's created a certain lifestyle for himself since he graduated, and he doesn't want to go back to supermarket meal deals and shared accommodation. But he also knows he isn't looking to hire more dentists. He loves working for himself, but that doesn't mean he wants to build an empire. He has friends running large companies, and the last thing he wants to worry about is juggling personalities or discussing KPIs in the Monday morning sales meeting. But if he's not sharing the workload, the question is, how can he buy back some time?

Neil decides to make a graph. He puts his customers in and thinks: *How can I free up some time and still make the same amount of money?* The answer becomes obvious: he must put his prices up. But Neil's smart; he's a dentist, after all, so he doesn't guess. It's time to zoom out and ask himself the right questions. *How many days a week do I want to work? How much do I want to earn? How much do I need?*

Neil's happy with his current paycheck. He wants

at least the same amount of money, but he also wants to take every Sunday off. So, he works out how many customers he needs to cull and recalculates his costs based on the new total. It makes for good reading. But how does he decide which customers to lose? Is it 'last in, first out?' Does he draw names in a raffle?

RULE OF THUMB

Let the price
increase cull the
customers you
no longer need.

No, like I said, Neil's smart; he has a plan for that, too. He goes through his customer base and works out the people who pay him the most and the ones he really enjoys talking to – those who make his work a pleasure. He's left with at least 20 people that don't fit either description; these are the "less desirables". These are people who often reschedule at the last minute, turn up late, and moan about every part of the process. It's not a tough decision. Naturally, he loses some customers because of the price increase anyway, but for any leftovers he still wants to shift, he contacts them with details of other practices they could try.

After the work is done, Neil is still making the same in turnover but he's also enjoying one day off a week and not dealing with as many problem clients. For a while, he's content with that. But a few years later, he's approaching 35, and his kids look at him like he's "A friend of mummy's" who sometimes stays for dinner. He's starting to want less from work and more from life.

As he's driving home from work that night, caught in the same traffic that has made him miss a hundred bedtime stories, he knows he's had enough. He hammers his fist into his steering wheel and his horn triggers a cacophony of angry beeps. When the noise finally dies down, he calls his wife.

"I'm…"

"Stuck in traffic? Yeah, yeah, I know," she says. "Your dinner's in the oven."

"Right," he replies.

"No, put that down," she yells, behind the sound of laughing kids and splashing bath water. "Do you need anything, babe? I've got my hands full here."

"5pm," he says.

"What about it?"

"From next month, that's when I'll be back."

"O... kay..." she says. "What day?"

"Every day!"

The silence between them is palpable, just for a moment, before it's sliced apart by the shrieks of heedless children. They both laugh.

"Well, okay," she says. "5pm!"

"5pm!"

He hangs up the phone and greedily swallows the five paces of tarmac that's opened up in front of him.

Same Questions, Different Answers

By the time Neil's in his early forties, he has a great relationship with his kids, his wife is back at work, and they're earning as much as they ever have. He loves his job, he always has, but he can't shake the feeling that he's still trading too much time for money. He's just bought a new set of golf clubs, and his goal for the year is to win a society meet and finally break a hundred. Once again, it's time to ask himself those familiar questions: *How many days a week do I want to work? How much do I want to earn? How much do I really need?*

He's noticed that every few years, the questions are the same, but the answers are slightly different. If he's going to fit in both his family *and* a new hobby, he really needs to work a four-day week. As he reflects, he realises he's never even taken the kids to school. How has that happened? He resolves to start work at 9:30am so he can drop them off at the front gate first. He'll need to put his prices up, and he'll no doubt lose some more customers, but it's nothing he hasn't done before. Neil's been following this process for almost 15 years. How does he do it, though? Why do his customers put up with it?

Building Trust

Imagine buying from the same person for over a decade. You build a level of trust and camaraderie that's hard to replicate, especially in a fast-paced digital world where everything is often so faceless.

Most people don't mind paying for a good plumber or mechanic; the price isn't really the issue. What they care about is not getting ripped off. They don't want to be made a fool of. They don't want to be sold four new tyres when all they needed was a pump. That feeling is magnified in healthcare. Whether the doctor throws you a box of Prozac just to get you out the door or the dentist sends you to the hygienist for the fifth time that year, you've put your trust in someone, and you just want to know you're getting honest advice. These customers have grown up alongside Neil and are likely earning more than they were previously. The price for everything has gone up, so why not their dentist?

Neil's also been laying foundations outside of his practice. He's been a member of the local trade organisation for many years and was recently put on the Committee for National Dentists. He even appears on podcasts and local TV when they need an expert. To an extent, it doesn't matter what he charges anymore; his reputation has earned him a waiting list for his services.

Eventually, Neil starts a YouTube channel. On his weekly show, he interviews patients live on air and helps them to overcome their dental problems and fears. The inaugural episode features two elderly patients.

The first is a lady, Kim, in her mid-60s. She's so terrified of the idea of a dentist she's never even been.

"I'll tell you what, Kim, I'm not going to use any instruments, but would it be okay to have a quick look in your mouth?"

"Ooh, I don't know," she replies.

"Well, it's up to you, of course, but we're here to help you overcome your fear. There's no dentist's chair. No tools. No lights. Just us." He lowers his voice. "And a small audience at home."

Kim laughs nervously. "Okay, Neil. Come on, then. Let's get it over with."

She opens her mouth, and Neil takes a preliminary look inside before sitting back down.

"See, that wasn't so bad, was it?"

Kim shakes her head. "No, but you didn't stick anything sharp in there," she replies.

Neil laughs. "So, it's the pain that worries you most?"

Kim nods sheepishly as Neil continues.

"Well, things have moved on a long way in the last few decades, Kim. I can get a hygienist to have another look for you; we can take some X-rays and assess the situation better, all without anything sharp."

"Okay," Kim says.

"If you get through that, we can move on to the next step, but if not, at least you know what's going on inside your mouth."

"And what's the next step?" she replies.

"Well, we have drops we can put on cotton wool; this numbs the area we're targeting. So, if we did want to inject anything, you wouldn't feel it. Then we can go to work. Again, only if you're ready."

Kim is growing in confidence and agrees to the X-rays.

Neil then turns to the next patient, a man in his 70s.

"And what about you, Peter? Has Kim inspired you to see a dentist?"

Peter's toothless smile reveals he's even more in need than Kim. "Oh no, no, no, no, no," he says.

"Okay," Neil replies. "Well, Kim's just made a huge step in the right direction. Do you have any questions for her? Perhaps you can share your experiences."

Peter thinks for a moment, pressing his gums into his lower lip. Eventually, he takes a deep breath and looks up. "Do you ever worry about appearanth?" he says.

Kim looks confused. "Oh, no!" she says. "My parents have been dead for years."

You can tell Neil's a seasoned professional because he manages to stop laughing almost as soon as he starts. "I'm hoping I can help with your appearance and your communication, Peter," he says.

Peter chuckles, and Neil goes on to assure him they can take it one step at a time, but if and when they finish, it will transform the quality of his life.

If Neil can help people like this, if he can be the person to get them in the chair after a lifetime of fear, they'll likely trust him with their money, their health, and even their grandkids. Needless to say, it's unlikely Kim or Peter would ever visit another dentist.

The lesson here is that if you build credibility as an expert in your field, it's much easier to charge what you like. Think of Michelin-starred restaurants. People are willing to make a reservation with them often without knowing anyone who has ever been.

Why? Because people trust the Michelin brand. Even if you've never heard of the place, when you see the star (or stars) in the window, it tells you a few things. You hope the service will match up to the food, but you *know* it won't be cheap. So, the brand is already telling you about portion sizes, the service, the cost and the environment.

If you want people to spend their money with you, it's imperative for your brand to build trust. Neil's done so much extra-curricular work over the years that his clients can sit around at dinner and brag about having one of the best dentists in the country.

"That sounds terrible, Keith! Let me put you in touch with Neil; he'll have you fixed up in no time."

"Oooh, I think my nephew sent me one of his videos the other day. What he did for those people was incredible."

And just like that, Neil has another customer.

All this extra work is starting to take its toll, though. Neil's in his 50s now, and he decides he'll only work Monday through Wednesday. He can return to working from 9am to 6pm because he has four days off in between, so he has more energy for longer days.

Things are going great until something dawns on him. He's been paying rent for his practice based on being there seven days a week. For years, though, he's been leaving it empty when he has days off. Not as smart as he thinks! So, he decides to sublet it to other dentists on the days he's not using it. That way, he more than offsets the cost of hiring it, but he's still not having to employ other dentists or getting involved in their business.

By the time he's in his 60s, he's very happy working a couple of days a week with people he likes, who always show up and are happy to pay the going rate.

There are lots of lessons to learn from Neil, but chiefly, to remember to take a step back. Neil was consistently able to zoom out, analyse his situation and figure out what he wanted before structuring his life around it. Whether you're an employee, a freelancer, or a business owner, work out what you want first, then crunch the numbers and figure out how to get there. If a dentist can get to this point, so can a coder, an accountant, or a graphic designer.

"Of course, a dentist can make £100,000 a year," I hear you say, "but I'm a copywriter; it's much harder for me."

Don't forget that Neil has a proprietary business. He can't sell it; there's no lump sum at the end to retire on because he IS the business. So, he has to make hay while the sun shines. You're a writer, but that doesn't mean you don't have options. You could merge with a graphic design agency and give your clients both images and words. You could hire a salesperson and other writers and take your approach to copywriting further afield. Not to mention, if you pen a popular book or TV show, you could cash in on the IP. When all is said and done, you could easily outperform Neil financially.

But let's say you have no desire to be a business owner, and you've never been interested in writing novels either; you help brands with their copy, and that's your thing. Rising to the top in any field will earn you the type of living most people can only dream of. It takes time, but look at Neil; he leaned in. He attended the committee meetings, was active with the trade organisations, and he moved with the times and got himself a YouTube channel.

Whether he's being active on social media, public speaking, or doing voluntary work in the local community, he's slowly but surely building his profile as an expert in his field. He didn't need to be the best, but he did need to be seen.

I've never heard anybody say to me, "I went to see a surgeon the other day, she specialises in hearts, apparently, but I can't find anything about her. I've looked her up, and there's nothing anywhere. But you know, she's cheap, so I took a punt."

If you work at a big agency with global customers and eye-watering budgets, are you really going to risk your high-profile clients on a copywriter you've never heard of, with no track record? You might, but it's unlikely. If you're hiring someone and they don't have a LinkedIn profile or a CV, in this day and age especially, you're probably going to think twice, aren't you? If you're going on a date with someone you met on an app and there's no other online presence of this person anywhere, that might be okay, sure, but it's something to think about.

Bill Gates said, "Most people *overestimate* what they can do in a year and *underestimate* what they can do in 10."

So, start now. Gradually build your profile, and as it increases incrementally, so can your pricing, until, eventually, you can start living the life you always dreamed of. You have to zoom out first, though, and figure out what those dreams actually are.

Why work seven days a week when you have kids and you want to watch them play football? Cut your cloth accordingly. What's your number? Maybe it's £100,000 a year, and that's all that matters. Or maybe you'd be content with £70,000 but with three days off a week and two holidays a year with the family.

Whatever your dream is, be more like Neil: Start with what you want and then figure out how to get there.

Chapter 8

Start With What You Want

I've met countless senior executives who could run successful companies if they put their minds to it, but very few do. Why?

Well, often, it's because they're restricted by a sparkly pair of golden handcuffs. The higher you get up the corporate ladder, the harder it is to escape. You've got a big house, three fancy cars, and a private education for the kids. Sure, you probably work more hours than you'd like, and your phone might interrupt the sanctity of the family dinner table some nights, but you keep doing the math, and even with the extra time you put in, your hourly rate is still worth every sacrifice.

So, when your old school buddy phones you up trying to tempt you into starting a business with him, you close your eyes and imagine what this new life would look like. No boss. No contracted hours. No being told where to be. It sounds fantastic.

But then the reality starts to dawn on you: No boss. No contracted hours. No being told where to be. The buck stops with you. You'd go from struggling to balance life and work to a life *defined* by your work. Instead of *making* money, you're *investing* it – you're paying wages, sick pay, and annual leave (for everybody but yourself). You've gone from receiving a monthly salary that would make your younger self jump with joy to a salary that would make him weep into his lunch box.

The absence of all those perks you've been enjoying for so long would leave a gaping hole in your lifestyle as you fund your own travel expenses, team drinks and even health insurance. Your security of tenure is replaced by uncertainty, and the conversations you're having with your financial adviser have taken a much less jovial tone.

You open your eyes and think, *Maybe now's not the right time.*

* * *

In terms of the best foundations for an entrepreneur, you're almost better off as a junior employee who decides to give running a business their best shot than being 20 years deep into a career where you're highly regarded and well paid, because it's almost impossible to imagine giving all that up. And, generally, people don't unless they're made redundant or get fired. Why would they leave?

My advice might surprise you: If you get the opportunity to thrive in corporate life, seize it with both hands. Enjoy it. Work hard and get the best income available to you. Self-employment isn't for everyone. It's for people who can't cope in corporate life. They either can't listen to another awful boss, or they have a passion so strong that it's worth all the uncertainty in time, money and opportunity.

When you start a company, *you're* the boss, and that's one of the most appealing things to most people. But, also, when you start a company, *you're* the boss, so you can't blame anyone else anymore.

To be candid, in the early days, you're probably not very good either. When you first do anything, really, how good are you? And yet you've got the responsibility of employing other people, funding their wages, motivating them and managing their days. You need to find customers, figure out how to charge them and apportion the tax. You might need to pay for IT, rent, insurance and, of course, yourself!

You'll uncover all sorts of strange job roles, like when you try a new sport and the next day you've got aches in muscles you never knew existed. Maybe your van breaks down, you're diagnosed with diabetes, your dad dies, or the dog has puppies, whatever the scenario, you still have to think about work. But in corporate life, you can switch off: you get compassionate leave and keep getting paid regardless.

None of this is to put you off. It's just to say that the high-paid corporate world can be very sticky, and breaking free from those golden handcuffs will unlock a totally different lifestyle, with both the good and the bad to consider.

Before You Start Your Business

People often ask me for a meeting so they can talk through their business ideas. They get the slides out, show me the branding, and pitch me the concept. They're usually very excited and can't quite work out why I'm not being pulled along in their slipstream.

If this is you, it's great you've jumped in and got started; that's the very essence of an entrepreneur: making things happen while others procrastinate. And if you've got this far in the book, I hope you've learned a lot about what's ahead.

However, before you go registering your name with Companies House and telling all your friends you're a CEO now, it's worth taking a moment's pause so we can zoom out and look at the bigger picture.

Have you asked yourself the right questions? Just because you have a business idea, and just because it can make money, doesn't mean it's the right decision for you. Do you even want a business? Or do you just want a job where you don't have a boss? Perhaps you're hoping to make your millions but haven't yet realised you're in the wrong industry. The more understanding you have about what you're trying to achieve, and what your goals are, the more you can build a business that points you in that direction.

You see, people often operate in the wrong order. They start trading, marketing and hiring before they've thought about what they want from their business, so they're constantly fighting to break out of the cage they've created for themselves.

So, what are the right questions?

Well, they're all about *you*. They should help you understand your own goals and motivations. After all, how can you steer a ship if you have no idea where it's going?

8 Questions You Must Have an Answer For

It's natural to feel excited when starting a company, and that's a good thing; channelling that positivity will attract the right kind of people to work with you. Just try not to get carried away and allow that nervous energy to fly in the face of solid foundations.

When someone asks me for advice about their new business, before we zoom in on the specifics, I always ask them the same questions. Take a few minutes to read them here and process your answers. Write them down if you want. If you're reading this on a train or a bus, take your phone out and put your thoughts in the notes, or email yourself so you can refer back to them.

Some of this might seem obvious, but I assure you, just the process of considering these things will put you in a much better place than when you started. When you've done this, talk to someone you trust. Tell them your plans. The power of giving a voice to the answers might just be the extra pull you need.

What do you want to achieve?
Do you want to make a ton of money and then move to the Caribbean? Or is it more about creating a legacy that lives beyond you? Do you simply want to be your own boss? Or do you want to start a family dynasty?

Are you passionate about your idea?
Do you love it? Is it already your hobby? Or does it feel like a task, a means to an end?

Do you want to be the only person working in the business?
Or do you want people you can collaborate with?

Do you want your family working in the business with you?
What about your friends? Is that a good idea? Or a bad one?

When do you want to retire?
Are you on the beach at 40, or will you go until the wheels fall off?

Will you take a salary?
If so, how much money do you want to make?

Where's your funding coming from?
Do you have investors? Will you borrow from the bank? Do you have personal guarantees to sign? Have you got clients paying already?

Do you want to exit one day?

Are you aiming to sell to a larger brand when you're in your 30s? Or are you picturing yourself at 60, floating your empire on the Stock Exchange?

* * *

Let's look at a couple of real-life examples. We'll start with Mary, a young woman launching an IT business. Mary is 35 years old, experienced in her field and a mother of two.

What do you want to achieve?

A solid business to support a nice home with my husband and kids. In the long term, I'd like a healthy work/life balance.

Are you passionate about the work?

Yeah, I love it, and I'm very good at it.

Do you want to be the only person working in the business?

I definitely want employees. I spend so much time working; business has to be a social thing, too.

What about family and friends? Could they work with you?
I'm not sure yet. I think I'll work with a friend initially and see how it goes. I can't imagine having to tell my sister what to do.

When do you want to retire?
No later than 60. But I'd like to be able to step back before then and spend more time with my kids.

Will you take a salary? If so, how much money do you want to make?
Yeah, at least 50k. I need to pay for schooling and baby care, and I want my kids to have what they need as they grow.

Where's the money coming from?
My husband and I have been saving, so we've agreed to use this to set up our future.

Do you want to exit one day?
Yes, unless the kids want to take over. Ideally, I'd like to make enough money to retire.

Mary isn't asking for anything unattainable; she has a good sense of what she wants and a supportive partner who can help supplement her income.

In truth, whilst the answers can be revealing, what *really* matters is that Mary *has* answers. When I sit with people and they can't reply to some of these questions, I always ask them one more: Are you sure you're ready for this?

* * *

Now, let's look at one of my businesses. I'll put myself in the shoes of 28-year-old me back in the late 1970s, when I had a spring in my step and a head full of hair. How would I have answered these questions then, I wonder?

What do you want to achieve?
A profitable business. I just want to earn more money working for myself than I would if I was employed by someone else.

Are you passionate about your work?
I love it, and not just the industry; I love *business*.

Do you want to be the only person working in the business?

Oh, I need employees. I'm not very good at a lot of tasks. I see myself learning how to do something and then employing people to do it better.

Do you want your family or friends working in the business with you?

Absolutely, yes.

When do you want to retire?

In my 60s.

Will you take a salary? If so, how much money do you want to make?

Yes, but as little as possible. I want to put the business in the strongest position I can.

Where's the money coming from?

I'm working in a casino in Iran and using my wages to supplement my business expenses. Once we have enough revenue, I'll fly back to the UK to take over.

Do you want to exit one day?
Absolutely, yes.

* * *

If you've read this far, you'll probably know that the business was called City Cruises. In 2019, we exited after almost 40 years of building the brand.

When we started, we had one floating fuel barge in an industry on the brink of collapse. When we walked away, we'd built the UK's largest tour boat company. I've mentioned a few times that we had a fleet of 40 vessels, but if you include all our pontoons, piers, mooring barges and work boats, we were closer to 50. At our peak, we reached four million annual passengers and a turnover of over £25 million. When I see that written down, I do know that it's a hell of an achievement. I should put my feet up, really. But anyone who knows me will agree that this is extremely unlikely.

Let's review some of my answers and see if they help to explain why I just can't keep my foot off the gas (and why you may not be able to either).

Was I passionate about it?

Very much so, and it certainly helped when I was dragging myself out of bed at 5am, especially when there was a stiff winter's breeze, and I knew I was going to be outside on a boat all day.

If your business is also your hobby, something you're good at, or something that brings happiness to others, it makes all the horrible, tough, painful decisions you'll have to make (and you will have to make them) that much easier to live with. It makes all those days of wondering whether to pay the heating bill or take that client for lunch much easier to stomach.

There's a saying that goes, 'Do what you love, and you'll never have to work a day in your life.' In my experience, that's not entirely true. Sometimes, even love is something you have to work on. For me, it's, 'Do what you love, and you'll never dream of a day without it.'

When did I want to retire?

Of course, I didn't have these questions when I was 28, so I never even considered retirement back then, but if you'd have asked me, maybe I'd have said in my 60s. To someone in their mid-20s, it's hard to look that far ahead and judge whether you'll still have the same zest for life. Of course, when you get there, you know it's less about zest and more about desperately clinging on to your health like a puppy refusing to let go of a tennis ball.

When you get past 60, it's as if three years pass every 12 months. When you're approaching 70, well, it's like living in dog years.

Age doesn't affect your desire, but it does take you longer to recover from a busy week; you can't work as many hours, and the way you interact with people changes. But for someone like me, who was always responsible for the vision of the company, you start to realise, *Hang on, I might not be around when this plan comes to fruition. We've got the next 20 years laid out, but I'll be grateful if I can still put my socks on by then, let alone run a business.*

By the time we publish this book, I'll have sailed past 70. I've had – by most people's metrics – huge success, and I certainly don't need to work anymore. So why do I? You might think I'm mad.

Well, for a start, what else am I going to do? Everyone says they want to retire early, but then what? Spend the next decade or two glued to a sun lounger until your skin feels like a horse's saddle and your own conversation finally bores you to death? As you can tell, that's not for me, but there is more to it than that.

RULE OF THUMB

Selling your business
isn't the end;
it's the start of
something new.

Business is about solving people's problems. If you do it well enough, people will pay handsomely, and you might just walk away with some money at the end. But even then, there's a whole new bunch of problems to solve: What do you do with your money? Do you leave it all in one place, or do you spread it around a bit? Do you keep it in the bank and claim the minimal interest each year? What will give you more protection? How do you leave it to your children without giving just as much to the taxman? Do you invest? What does that even mean? Of course, we know what the definition is, but what does it mean for your liabilities, your free time, and your golf handicap?

We all have these grandiose plans of making a

million in our 40s and then kicking back in a hot tub with a Piña Colada for the rest of our days, but when you have the money, that's when the real work begins. You're now part of a scary new world where you have to learn financial buzzwords and what they mean for your future. You have to work out who's trying to help you solve your problems and who's just trying to move *your* money to *their* bank account.

Even if you *don't* reinvest, you have to manage your estate; it's not quite the work-free retirement you might have imagined when you were young. In truth, on the day we sold our company, we were very much back in business.

A family business?

For me, this was a no-brainer. I've seen many couples over the years become like passing ships in the night because of their work schedules. I've witnessed wonderful people become parents who work so hard they never see their kids. My dad was one of them. I only started working on the River Thames because I wouldn't have seen him otherwise. Perhaps that stuck with me. I knew I'd be working every hour I could stand up straight, for decades, so it made sense to bring the family on the journey with me.

With my wife, Rita, at my side, and my children, Lucy and Matthew, both playing a part, it was the only way I could find the balance to make both parts of my life work in harmony.

Would I take a salary?

As little as possible is probably a fairly unpopular answer to most people reading this. Perhaps it's my humble roots, but even from a young age, I didn't need much. I wanted to be the poorest employee and make sure I was putting as little strain on the business as possible.

My mindset was always that I was an employee, but instead of taking my wages, I was taking shares. So, even at the height of City Cruises, instead of a 70k package with all the bells and whistles, I was taking more like 40k. If and when we'd get to a position to sell, that's when I'd see my return.

Did I want to exit?

Even back then I knew that I wanted to exit the company one day. I had no idea what that looked like, just that I had to work towards removing myself from it. Rita joining me was the first step to implementing policies and procedures that turned us into a grown-up business. From then on, everything we did and every decision we made had to have the exit in mind, even if it was just a shimmering star on the horizon. My mantra was to *stay* ready so that when the time came, I didn't have to *get* ready.

A Company or a Business?

Now what? Let's say you're 20 and you want to retire at 50 with a million pounds after tax. Great! We now know what we're aiming for in terms of turnover, profit and how much time you have to get there. Then, we must work out what the business is going to be, what it's called, how it makes money, and how much you want to earn.

Knowing what you want from the beginning will not only light the path for you to travel down but also help you to discover whether it's the right decision in the first place. Imagine being three years into your business before you think about whether you even want to be an entrepreneur.

Perhaps you're one of those people who just doesn't want to work for someone else anymore. You're tired of temperamental bosses dictating your progress, having to ask for holidays, and working long hours for the same reward.

Don't panic! There are more options than you think. We can build you a job that will give you the fulfilment you're looking for. Much like a freelancer, you can run a small operation, choose your own hours, and, eventually, even pick the types of clients you want to work with. Just ask Neil, the dentist.

Alternatively, your goals could be to grow a huge business, manage teams of people, and one day exit to a larger company. If this is you, it's vital to remember that just because you own a company doesn't mean you're running a business. Yes, you read that right!

RULE OF THUMB

Just because you own a company, doesn't mean you're running a business.

Most owners like to think that because they have a company, they have something they can sell one day, but in the vast majority of cases, they don't. There are many reasons why this might be, but one major factor is that often these people don't have a business; they have a job.

That's not a bad thing. A job where you get to choose your own hours, make the decisions, be creative and earn great money is fantastic, inspiring even; it just isn't a business.

So, how can we tell the difference?

Working ON it Versus Working IN it!

Are you buried in the day-to-day, unable to work ON the business because you're too busy working IN it? This is very common in a startup, of course, because when you begin, you're doing all the roles yourself.

You may be able to muddle your way through the company accounts in the first year or two, but as you grow to six or seven figures in turnover, you're unlikely to have the time or the skills to do it effectively.

You can run your social media profiles for a while until you realise it's taking too much of your time away from sales, people management, or delivery of the product. Not to mention, it might just not be your bag. If you thought you were on FaceTime for 15 minutes before you realised it was an Instagram Live, maybe you should leave the socials to someone who won't accidentally broadcast themselves in the bath (as quickly as possible).

A new company is like a leaking boat; there are holes everywhere, and you have to work like crazy to plug as many as you can until someone can come along and fix them. You always have to work on getting yourself out of these temporary positions as quickly as possible so you can move on to the next gap in the company, fulfil that role, and then fill it with a professional.

The good news is that when you do go to hire people, you know exactly what you're looking for because you've actually done the job. It becomes easier to hold people accountable because when they say, "That's not possible", you can reply, "Not only is it possible, I managed to do it while I was also working in four other roles simultaneously. I even did an Instagram Live once."

Once you've plugged enough holes, it's time to come up for air and work ON the business. This means focusing on the bigger picture and analysing the whole instead of getting bogged down in the details. It's picking a direction. By this point, you might even have a captain, someone steering the ship, but *you* are the one who plots the course. You've got to give yourself time to strategise, evaluate and create the vision.

Could One Accident Kill You AND the Business?

Perhaps the best way to tell if you have a business is to remove yourself from the equation. If you're the owner and we took you out of the operations today, would it still run? Do your customers still get what they've been promised? Do your staff get paid? Or does the ship slowly start to sink?

Once again, selling or dying, it's the same problem. The business still has to run in your absence. One way or another, we all exit at some point. So, you must build something that operates on its own – whether you're on holiday, off sick, or, heaven forbid, you get hit by a bus. If it thrives with or without you working in it, only then do you have something to sell; only then do you have a business.

Now, I know what some of you are thinking: *I can get there when the time comes.*

Whilst it isn't impossible to pull it all together at the last minute, it will certainly delay what you're trying to achieve and no doubt drive the price down. The longer you've been around (and the bigger you are), the harder it will be to retroactively build infrastructure. Imagine trying to sort out the foundations of a house *after* you've built it. In most cases, you may as well just knock it down and start again.

RULE OF THUMB

Don't wait until you want to sell to get all your ducks in a row.

If you start your business with the end in mind, you can take steps each day, however tiny, that will add zeros to your sale price.

Three Things Every Entrepreneur Should Think About

As a new business owner, you'll have so much on your mind. When you hear more seasoned entrepreneurs say they're constantly spinning plates, wearing different hats, and burning the midnight oil, you'll suddenly understand what they mean.

And as you're desperately dodging a dozen clichés a day (and doing your best to avoid becoming one yourself), it can seem almost impossible to know where to focus.

Strip away the fluff – zero in on what's important.

1. Health
2. Business acumen
3. Profit

If you can prioritise these three things, you'll give yourself and your business the best chance of success.

Health

You don't need me to tell you how important your health is. Life and time are the best teachers you'll ever have. What I can tell you is how important it is to have processes in place that mean you and your staff don't have to choose between work and health; these should never be mutually exclusive.

Gone are the days when company culture could be defined by 4pm finishes on a Friday and boozy lunchtimes in the local pub. If you want to reward your staff, why not give them something they'll remember in the years to come or (hear me out) that improves the quality of their lives?

RULE OF THUMB

If you don't make time for health, you make time for illness.

You might already subsidise a local gym membership, but how supportive are you when they use it? Could you extend lunch breaks by 15 minutes three times a week, so your staff can shower and eat after exercising? Maybe they could start and finish later so they can add an early yoga class to their routine. Are there local five-a-side football or netball leagues your company could join? If so, could you sponsor their kits and cover the entry fee?

As your business grows, you must consider what benefits will attract the top talent. What do people worry about? How can you get them to work happy and healthy? How about medical insurance that covers dental work, injuries and therapy? Can you include their immediate families in the plan?

Imagine how distracted they'll be at their desk if their spouse or children desperately need an MRI, but they're told they have to wait between six and 18 weeks.

When you're young, you think you're invincible, but as you get older, the fear starts to set in, and you begin thinking about how to undo all the damage you've put yourself through. Every year, I get an MOT through BUPA. They check my body fat percentage and my blood pressure, test me for diabetes and assess my lung age. Knowing what's going on inside you and having experts on hand to help you improve gives you a welcome peace of mind for the next 12 months. Once we started to offer this to our staff, a culture of education and knowledge sharing grew, with open conversations about mental and physical health. For me, these are the things you can call tangible benefits. They might be why people join your company over a competitor and could be a consideration in why they stay.

A fridge full of booze isn't a benefit; for some people, it's not even a perk. If you count the Christmas party as a benefit and then make people come in on a Saturday to attend it, don't be surprised if there's less excitement than expected.

RULE of THUMB

Don't build
your celebration
(or any event)
around free drinks.

"Where's the Christmas party this year, Eric?"

"We'll probably just hire the same room as last year, I think."

"Any entertainment?"

"Of course! There's a free Jägerbomb bar at the front!"

"Oh, okay, brilliant. Should we get a DJ as well?"

"Er, yeah, could do, I suppose."

I hate to break it to you, but if your main attraction is free alcohol, you're doing it wrong. You must have a pull beyond getting trashed with your colleagues. That's not to say you can't go to a bar and cut loose, but once again, you shouldn't make people choose between work and health. What if they don't want to drink? What if they're driving, in recovery, or don't fancy losing another weekend to a pounding headache and a bucket load of existential dread?

If you have three draught beers, a rack of spirits, and half a dozen cocktails on the menu, what are you saying to the non-drinkers when they can choose from Becks Blue, water or a Virgin Mojito? It's like plonking a bowl of salad leaves in front of a vegetarian and saying, "It's your fault for not eating meat." Because that's exactly what it feels like: a punishment.

Health and wellness should be encouraged with the same vigour that strip bars and drinking competitions were in the '80s and '90s. If your sales team knocks it out of the park, celebrate with remarkable experiences, not by revisiting the same old nightclub before sending them back to their families barely able to string a sentence together.

It comes from the top. What you do as a leader will be an example that many of your team will follow. If you work hard, turn up on time, and care for yourself, that will become the culture. But if you're boozing until the early hours, turning up late and constantly dipping into petty cash, what do you think your managers will do? If they're not allowed to do as you do, they won't have the respect to do as you say.

Business acumen

A huge number of businesses fail in their first five years. If four friends each start their own company today, the chances are only one of them will still be trading a decade later. But what I find just as fascinating is how many businesses survive these bleak statistics only to get stuck in the mud. They exist in the same form for years, unable to get past 40 or 50 staff or move beyond their £1 million in turnover to, say, £5 million.

RULE OF THUMB

What got you here won't get you there.

It's common for owners to reach a moderate amount of business success – an okay salary, decent car, 40 staff, 10 years of trading behind them – but then they just stop growing. No matter what they do, they can't seem to break through to that next level.

If you've stopped growing externally, there's a high chance you've stopped growing internally, too. How often do you ask for advice? Who's your business mentor? How often do you sit with your non-exec directors? Do you attend talks by people in that next phase up from you? And, more importantly, do you *listen*? Do you swallow the ego and take what they're saying on board?

* * *

Jason has been running his creative agency for over a decade. The company's been trading for 20 years and was passed down from a mother to her son, along with her wicked sense of humour and hardcore work ethic. The business has thrived where others have failed, in large part due to a willingness to work harder and for longer hours than anybody else. Unsurprisingly, this ethos has rooted itself in the company culture, where people are expected to clock up back-to-back 18-hour days at the drop of a hat. You're celebrated when you dig in and help the cause, even if that means working outside your job description. But you're shamed if you don't toe the line, or heaven forbid, ask for six hours between shifts.

If your business falls into this category, I can assume a few things: You find it difficult to recruit top talent, and you're constantly in a hiring phase. No doubt there's a mass exodus every 12 to 18 months, as whole departments leave within weeks of each other.

"I just can't seem to find the right people! The work ethic of these kids today," Jason says, shaking his head behind his fourth cappuccino of the day.

"Why do you think they keep leaving?" I ask, fighting the urge not to rattle off a list of reasons that are nestled on the end of my tongue.

"I dunno. Nobody wants to work for it anymore. It's the nature of the business; sometimes, you have to work long hours and put in hard graft."

"You can't expect your employees to pour their lives into *your* dream, though," I say. "Why would they work themselves to death for the same pay?"

"Don't give me that, Gary; I've read your first book; you're just as guilty as me."

"Sure," I say, "I put in the hours, but I was building my dream. I wasn't asking Jenny from accounts to jump in the van and help with deliveries all weekend."

Jason chuckles, but I could tell he still wasn't convinced.

"Whatever happens," I say, "you're smart enough to know you can't keep doing the same things and expect different results."

I checked back in with Jason a year or two later. He'd made sweeping changes in the following months. He started reading more business books, listening to podcasts and implementing new processes. He introduced hybrid working, let people leave early on a Friday, and ring-fenced people's times so there were at least nine hours between shifts.

Unfortunately, by the time we reconnected, it had all fallen apart. Revenue had decreased for a few months, so he fired the sales director. A few weeks later, the operations director resigned along with half his team, and the remaining staff were back to working five days a week in the office.

When we experience stress, we instinctively return to what we know best. Think of it like a compass that always points back north. If you're a grinder, someone who works long hours and pushes themselves to the brink, that's where you'll go when the tough times come. If you're an avid learner, perhaps you'll gravitate to mentors, books, or lessons from the past. It's in these times we need to be able to step away most, zoom out and recalibrate.

You have to look at yourself first. You can't just say, "Good staff are impossible to find these days," and then plod along for another five years with your eyes closed. Why can't you make it work? Assess your infrastructure, processes, HR and company culture.

Have you done all you can to give your company the best possible chance of success?

If you still don't know where to turn, hire someone who does. Invest in your future. Sacrifice some of your income now so you can grow it considerably in a few years.

RULE OF THUMB

The learning
never stops.

What can YOU do better? Do you micro-manage too much? Do you talk down to your staff and shame them in front of others? Are you expecting more than people are willing to give? Do you even know where your skill sets begin and end?

I reached my peak early on in most positions. I knew I'd find someone better at sales, marketing, social media, customer relations. As soon as I could, I hired people to replace me, and I moved on. I joined business clubs and attended seminars. I never got to the point where I thought, *I'm CEO, I'm right, everyone else is wrong.* If anything, I went too far the other way. I was always convinced I didn't know enough. I guess I was happy to be a beginner, bringing in experts and taking their advice. As Richard Branson says, you hire people to tell you what to do, not the other way around.

If I had thought someone else could grow the business better than me, I'd have resigned as CEO and just sat on the board. You have to know your limitations. When it became clear that I couldn't grow the business any further, it was a key factor in our decision to sell.

Think of it like Lloyds Bank: The CEO, the chairman and the bank teller – they might all have shares, but none of them own it, do they? They're all employees.

You should act as if you have an employment contract like everybody else. Turn up when you're supposed to, be kind and supportive to your colleagues, take your allocated time for lunch, fill in your expenses and hold yourself accountable. Live by the rule that if your employees shouldn't do it, neither should you.

RULE OF THUMB

Treat yourself as
an employee.

If you act like you have a contract (maybe even give yourself one), unsurprisingly, you'll probably be a good employee.

Profit

When do you become successful? Well, people have varying definitions of success. It might be waking up and doing something you love every day, or winning a big project you've always had your sights set on. I guess what most people mean when they ask me this question is, "When did you get to a point where you were financially comfortable?"

Anyone can get a big deal and have cash on the hip for a few weeks or months. But the key to this kind of success is consistency. It's the day you're not panicking about the bills you've got coming in, and you no longer feel guilty when you buy a coffee in the morning.

In truth, it came without warning. I had already been there for a while before I realised. I've always pictured success as an invisible line I needed to reach. It's like driving up a spiral ramp in a car park, going round and round in circles, waiting to pass the correct floor. You know you're going up, but you're never quite sure if it's enough until you exit and take a look around. Maybe you could have parked on the floor below or even further down, but it doesn't matter anymore; you're here now.

If you treat the business as your own personal cash machine, you may be driving flash cars and flying first class to your 40th birthday in the Maldives, but there will be no longevity. You have to keep the business in a healthy position. Treat it like a shareholder. It might be painfully slow, but if you're diligent, you can build up a healthy cash reserve. As your turnover grows and you understand the business more, you start to run the place more efficiently and increase your profit margins by a few per cent. Then you have some momentum.

In the early days, you're constantly juggling cash, getting paid by a client, and paying off old invoices with it. Eventually, you can start trading with your own money, but then new problems will arise. It's so hard to scale up using your cash flow, and if you're reinvesting all your profit into growth, you're leaving yourself extremely vulnerable. I know because, in the early days of City Cruises, no one would lend us any money. For many years, we had to pour all our resources into buying new assets.

Many small business owners will approach family and friends to invest. That's a lot of stress to have on your conscience, though. You have to be extremely confident in what you're offering. As for the banks, if you have a strong plan, they might back you, but they'll demand the money back, and if you don't pay, they'll close you down (and maybe take your house with it). It's a balancing act.

RULE OF THUMB

When you borrow
you must aim
for profit in the
short term.

When you ask for money, you need to have a plan for both short- and long-term returns. There's no use forecasting profits you won't see for a decade; how will you pay the loans back? Think of it like a credit card. At the very least, you must pay back the interest on the money you borrow, even if you can't pay back the capital. So long as you don't break the conditions of the loan, the bank will leave you to it.

RULE OF THUMB

Try to keep a year's worth of interest in the bank.

I've mentioned several times in this book that for us to build a new boat and get it to market was a seven-year project. But when you're including the finance, it's more like 14 years. It took seven years to plan and build and a further seven years to repay the loans. Most businesses don't even last that long. At one point, we built four boats simultaneously for several million pounds. When you're borrowing vast sums of money, the interest can hammer you. In our industry, it would only take one summer of bad weather and we'd suddenly be in a very precarious position.

There were some scary times for us, but we had a keen eye on the budget, and our disaster fund included a year's interest on our loans.

The idea of having new boats was to increase our income. It would have been catastrophic if we finally got them on the river only to make the same amount of money as in previous years. How would we pay back all that debt? We wanted bigger, contemporary and luxurious vessels to hold more people and give them the best experience on the river.

We replaced our old 200-seater boats with state-of-the-art ships, each with a capacity of 500. That's an extra 1,200 passengers across the four new builds (in both directions). When you're confident there's a market for your product, a decision like this seems like a no-brainer. Over a period of around 15 years, we managed to raise enough capital to increase our capacity by around 10,000 people per day. You come to realise that everything in business is a gamble. All you can do is identify the risks and prepare accordingly.

RULE OF THUMB

Prepare for bad
weather and pray
for sunshine.

A sightseeing business is seasonal, so we weren't reaching capacity in the winter months. As the saying goes, we had to make hay while the sun shined. There were roughly 26 weekends a year where we saw no increase over the original passenger numbers. The other 26, mixed in with the summer weekdays, were where we managed to pay back the loans.

For us, that was the risk: could we make enough in the busier times? Were we good enough to maximise profit when our overheads were much higher and our operations were constantly stretched to capacity?

When we won the Millennium Dome contract in 2000, our turnover went from £3 million to £7 million overnight. It takes a different type of business to succeed in this kind of environment, and we had to become experts in dealing with waves of customers.

Imagine opening a new restaurant in somewhere like the O2 Arena. It's going to be a vastly different operation to your other sites in Hackney and the West End. Even if you have loyal customers, it's unlikely they'll want to travel to a hectic venue like O2 when they can just visit you at your other locations. The bulk of your guests will come from people attending the shows in the auditorium. You might be lucky to get 30% occupancy most of the week, and then Taylor Swift headlines, and BOOM, you're fully booked four nights in a row, with people queuing around the corner. The staff have gone from finding things to do to barely having time to wipe the tables down between diners. You have to be at the very top of your game to survive.

Our summers were like a four-month run of nonstop arena shows. Even with the extra capacity, we knew we'd still be overflowing with people. It grew so much that we had to reconsider our entire partner strategy. We decided we could no longer work with tour operators who only brought us customers in peak season. We needed help from companies that could bring us passengers all year round. Even if it meant making less margin per ticket, the overall strength of the business would improve.

Reflecting on my life in business while writing

these books, it's clear that I spent the majority of my career building infrastructure. There were times when I thought the whole thing could collapse, but we made it through, partly because my focus never shifted: Prioritise health, keep learning, and pay off the loans.

Author's Note

In the 1970s, there was no test you had to pass to become a company director, no required learning, and 50 years on, there still isn't. I'm not here to argue whether that should be a legal requirement or not. I certainly don't think a degree or higher education is the only way to add value to the workplace. All I can say with confidence is that if there had been the option to do so, you can bet I'd have the certificate.

My entrepreneurial journey began with a good idea and commitment to a vision, but building solid foundations is where the profit came from, how we managed to exit on our own terms, and why I can sit here today and share these lessons with you.

With the right application of the principles in this book and perhaps some fortunate timing along the way, I hope you manage to build your dreams, and that these lessons stay with you, ready to pass on to the next generation of entrepreneurs who need to hear them.

Good luck, and thanks for reading.

For access to further resources, including our 7-day fast-track course, scan the QR code below or visit:

garybeckwith.com/millions-resources

Appendix (Rules of Thumb)

Preface

- Winning doesn't always indicate success.

HR

Job Descriptions:

- Every duty requiring attention should be in somebody's job description.

The Joys of Recruitment:

- Never hire alone.
- Never employ in your own image.

The Interview Process:

- Make your interview questions the same for everybody.

Staff Retention:

- It all starts with the job description.
- Communicate early.

Wage Reviews:

- Don't (ever) make it up.

The Departure Lounge:

- If you fire someone it's your fault.

Psychometric Testing:

- Psychometric testing turns personalities into teamwork.

Infrastructure

Staffing levels:

- If you need 500 people, hire 512 instead.
- You recruit better when you're not panicking.
- Every employee should generate £100,000 t/o.

Physical Infrastructure:

- Shop for the future.

Online Infrastructure:

- Don't guess.
- The stronger the information, the better the decisions.
- Either you innovate or the market does it for you.

Processes:

- If you don't write it down, it doesn't exist.

More Than Just a Suggestion:

- Talk to your employees.

Health & Safety:

- Every part of your customers' journey is your problem.

Managing Money

Budgets:

- Every company needs a budget.
- Budgets should be monitored daily.

Cash Flow:

- Don't have lines that never move.

The Disaster Fund:

- You need a disaster fund.

Critical Financial Distress:

- A contract is only worth what you can enforce.
- Don't be afraid to ask for help.
- If you can see it happening, don't wait.

Buying and Selling

Incremental business:

- Incremental business doesn't work.

Evaluating stock:

- Assume you're paying a new price every day.

How to Exit a Business

How to Value Your Business:

- Highlight where the growth is happening.
- You must know the numbers.
- To get the best deal, you need a better story.

Stay ready:

- Trust your team and the buyer will as well.
- Selling or dying is the same problem.
- Plan for success with succession planning.

You've made your money... Now what?:

- Every decision you make in business must have tax in the equation.

How to Buy a Business

How to Buy a Business:

- Have a rule of thumb.
- Get more opinions.

Best Laid Plans:

- There are four ways to grow your business.

How to Grow a Business

How to Buy a Business:

- Processes are a friend to business.

Acquisitions:

- The environment of a business will often dictate how large it can grow.

The Dentist Theory:

- Let the price increase cull the customers you no longer need.

Start With What You Want

8 Questions You Must Have an Answer For:

- Selling your business isn't the end; it's the start of learning something new.

A Company or a Business?:

- Just because you own a company, doesn't mean you're running a business.
- Don't wait until you want to sell to get your ducks in a row.

Things to Think About:

- If you don't make time for health, you'll make time for illness.
- Don't build your celebration (or any event) around free drinks.
- What got you here won't always get you there.
- The learning never stops.
- Treat yourself as an employee.
- When you borrow you must aim for profit in the short term.
- Try to keep a year's worth of interest in the bank.
- Prepare for bad weather and pray for sunshine.

Acknowledgments

And now for some thank yous...

Thank you to Rita, Matthew and Lucy for your years of support.

Thank you to Stuart Groves for once again helping me translate dyslexic cockney and share my knowledge.

Thank you to our early readers who helped us shape the final version of the book: Colin Atkins, Dave Enderson, Steve Groves, Kelly Strong and Mary Follett.

And thank you to Danielle and Kinga for helping us get it out to the world.

About the Author

Gary Beckwith is a pioneering British entrepreneur. From leaving school at 15 with undiagnosed dyslexia and zero qualifications, he went on to build an empire on the River Thames.

Gary launched City Cruises PLC, a single vessel selling fuel to passing ships. Over the next four decades, working alongside his wife, Rita, that vessel became a fleet of 40, offering sightseeing, private charters, speed boat trips and more, in places like London, York and Poole. When they sold the business in 2019, it was carrying more than four million passengers a year, with over 500 staff, and generating an annual revenue of over £25 million.

Gary's success benefited more than just the Beckwiths. Thanks to their tireless lobbying, they secured a 10-year operating licence on the Thames, revolutionising the sector and enabling year-round planning, investment and growth.

In 2016, Gary was awarded an honorary Doctorate of Business Administration from Coventry University, and in 2019, he and Rita were inducted into the British Travel and Hospitality Hall of Fame. Gary's leadership and entrepreneurial story has been featured in major outlets, including *The Times*, *Forbes*, *Elite Business Magazine* and *Authority Magazine*.

In 2025, Gary released his debut book, *How to Make a Million in Business* (Wrate's Publishing), which blends his extraordinary personal story with practical lessons for entrepreneurs. The book has been praised as "a fascinating look back on 50 years of hard graft, distilled into lessons that can help and inspire the next generation of entrepreneurs" (*Elite Business*). And

The Times said, "There may not be anybody alive who knows the River Thames better than Gary Beckwith."

Today, Gary continues to invest in businesses, mentor entrepreneurs through online courses and share his insights as a speaker and author.

Also by Gary Beckwith

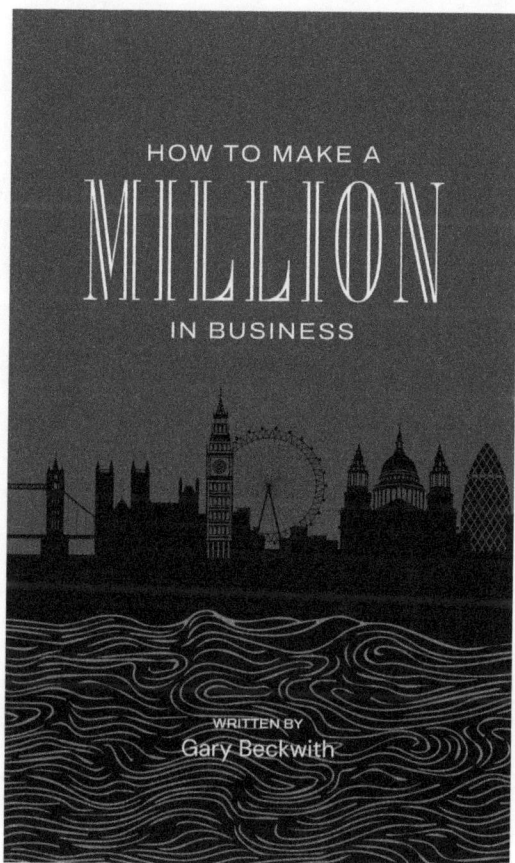

HOW TO MAKE A

MILLION

IN BUSINESS

WRITTEN BY
Gary Beckwith

www.ingramcontent.com/pod-product-compliance
Lightning Source LLC
Chambersburg PA
CBHW030452210326
41597CB00013B/640